Living a Joyous Life

BOOKS BY RABBI DAVID AARON

Endless Light: The Ancient Path of the Kabbalah to Love,
Spiritual Growth, and Personal Power

Inviting God In: Celebrating the Soul-Meaning
of the Jewish Holy Days

Living a Joyous Life:
The True Spirit of Jewish Practice

The Secret Life of God:
Discovering the Divine within You

Seeing God: Ten Life-Changing Lessons
of the Kabbalah

Living a Joyous Life

THE TRUE SPIRIT OF JEWISH PRACTICE

Rabbi David Aaron

TRUMPETER

BOSTON & LONDON

2007

Trumpeter Books
An imprint of Shambhala Publications, Inc.
Horticultural Hall
300 Massachusetts Avenue
Boston, Massachusetts 02115
www.shambhala.com

9 8 7 6 5 4 3 2 1

First Edition

Printed in the United States of America

♾ This edition is printed on acid-free paper that meets the
American National Standards Institute Z39.48 Standard.

Distributed in the United States by Random House, Inc.,
and in Canada by Random House of Canada Ltd

Library of Congress Cataloging-in-Publication Data
Aaron, David, 1957–
Living a joyous life: the true spirit of Jewish practice/
David Aaron.—1st ed.
p. cm.
ISBN-13: 978-1-59030-395-5 (alk. paper)
1. Spiritual life—Judaism. 2. Judaism—Customs and practices.
3. Joy—Religious aspects—Judaism. 4. God (Judaism) I. Title.
BM723.A185 2007
296.7—dc22
2006103019

❖ ❖ ❖

Special thanks to my true friend Dr. Herb Caskey,
whose generosity made this project possible.
May the study of this book bring
great merit to his parents,
Morris and Rose Caskey of blessed memory

❖ ❖ ❖

To my parents Joseph and Luba
To my wife Chana
To my children Lyadya, Aharon, Neema,
Yisroel, Annaniel, Nuriel, Yehuda,
Tzuriel, and Shmaya
To my grandchildren Nachalya and Shira
Thank you for your very sweet love!

Contents

Acknowledgments

GREAT THANKS to my wife, Chana. May each day of our lives be a joyous and constant celebration of our love for God, each other, our parents, children, grandchildren, and all people.

Many, many thanks to my very talented editor, Elicia Mendlowitz, who did an exceptional job helping me put these ideas into writing. I am also very thankful to Uriela Sagiv for adding her professional touch, giving these ideas even greater clarity.

My deep appreciation to Beth Frankl of Trumpeter Publications for her expertise and advice.

I am extremely grateful to the many friends and supporters of Isralight International, whose generosity has provided me with the opportunity to present the ideas in this book. Special thanks to Dr. Herb and Irena Caskey, Robby and Helene Rothenberg, Andrew and Shannon Penson, Dr. Michael and Jackie Abels, George and Pam Rohr, David and Dena Reiss, Robyn Barsky, Tzvi Fishman, and Steve Eisenberg for their consistent love and support.

I am also grateful to the many students who have attended my talks, Isralight seminars, and retreats. Your questions, challenges, and receptivity have brought me much blessing and inspiration.

I am forever in debt to my holy teachers, especially Rabbi Shlomo Fischer *shlita,* for all their brilliance and warmth.

Thank you, God. My entire being is filled with joy and gratitude to serve You.

David Aaron
Old City, Jerusalem

LIVING A JOYOUS LIFE

Introduction

MY FATHER was born in Russia, into a very religious family. In fact, my grandfather—my *zeide*—was so religious that people in his village would say, "If Laibl does it, then it's okay." Drafted into the Russian army, from which no one ever seemed to get out, my father looked for an escape, and he found a way. But before he took the momentous step of deserting the Russian army to flee to North America, he wrote a letter to his father, my *zeide*, explaining his plan and asking whether he should do it. My *zeide* told my father, "I would rather have satisfaction from a distance than pain up close."

Then he said something powerful: "Please, my son, remember that you are a Jew. Please, my son, remember to keep Jewish law always." My father promised my *zeide* that he would remember, but when he got to Canada and struggled to make a living, he decided he needed to give up his commitment to Shabbat, and with that the rest of his Jewish observance slowly dissipated.

So I did not grow up with a very strong Jewish background. Of course, we went to synagogue for Rosh Hashanah and Yom Kippur. And we ate a festive Passover meal, but there was no regular expression of Jewish life. We didn't keep kosher or celebrate Shabbat in our home. However, I did know that I was

Jewish, because my mother is a Holocaust survivor. And I knew that a large group of people in the world hated me, because I was a Jew. But I didn't know *why* I was a Jew. And I knew that if I had been born fifty years earlier, I too might have died in a concentration camp, as did most of my mother's family.

None of the above seemed like a good reason to want to be Jewish. So I grew up knowing that I was Jewish, but I didn't have many positive feelings about being a Jew. I was a Jew by guilt.

Although I had little real knowledge of Judaism, I had a very negative feeling about what I did know—like the bit about being "chosen."

When I was very young, my parents told me that I was part of the "chosen people" and, because of that, I had been "chosen" to study in Hebrew school for two hours every day after regular school. As you can imagine, I did not feel great about being chosen. All of my friends left school at three o'clock, at which time they went home to watch *Batman* or *Superman* or *Bugs Bunny* on TV. Meanwhile, I had to read a book about Moses and Aaron splitting the Red Sea. In my childhood mind, Moses and Aaron were not impressive. Superman could have picked the Israelites up and flown them over that sea. The Torah giants were no superheroes to me.

Hebrew school was boring. It was there that I learned how to roll a spitball. Otherwise, I stared out the window and day-dreamed. I must admit, however, that Hebrew school actually gave me a certain faith in God. Every day I would sit there bored out of my mind, with no other choice but to pray. "Please

God, You took the Jewish people out of Egypt. Can't you take me out of Hebrew school?"

Thank God, my bar mitzvah came. Now I knew I would be a free man, free of Hebrew school and most things Jewish.

It was not until I turned 18 that I decided, following the example of my sister, to explore authentic Judaism. I went to Israel to study for one year, and I enjoyed it so much that I wrote my parents a letter asking them if I could stay another year. This was a stroke of genius, because I was such a rebellious kid that I would have generally said, "Guess what, I'm staying!" But maturity entered into my head for some reason, and I wrote them and asked for permission. Of course, if they had said no I wouldn't have listened. But I figured that it would be the right thing to ask my parents for their blessings. The shock was that my parents said yes. My father wrote me a very touching response:

Dear David,

When I was a child, all that my father wanted from me was to learn in a yeshiva. Your *zeide* was a poor shoemaker, and all he dreamed about was that I would go to yeshiva and maybe become a rabbi. Here, my own son, who's named after my father, is asking me to learn in a yeshiva. How can I say no to my son?

It's a moving personal story, but it is also the drama of the Jewish people in general.

What happened from my *zeide's* time till my time? What broke down in the chain of tradition?

I believe that the central problem was, and continues to be, a lack of understanding of the spiritual meaning of Judaism and the joy in living Jewish. We need to know the *why's* of being Jewish. If we don't understand what Judaism means, then we can't really love it, and we are not going to live it. It's not enough for rabbis or parents to tell us that we *should* be Jewish. People don't always do what they *should* do. But most people do what they love to do. It would be great if we could love to do what we should do.

Most Jews don't love being Jewish because they don't understand who they are or why they would want to live what Judaism teaches. If you don't know yourself, your traditions, or your history, then you can't know your reason for living as a Jew. If you don't know yourself, you can't love yourself. But love depends on a connection. Most Jews are not connected to their Jewish identity, and this is why they don't love being Jewish.

Very often people think that Judaism can be approached in a linear way—you ask a question and get an answer. For this reason, I generally have a hard time with free-for-all "ask the rabbi" formats. Here's why:

Let's say a person asks, "Rabbi, why do Jews celebrate Shabbat?" I'd have to answer the question from a holistic point of view. For me to explain why we celebrate Shabbat, I first would have to talk about creation, because Shabbat is related to the creation story—in six days God created the world, on the seventh day God rested. But before I could talk about creation, I would have to talk about what it means that God creates at all. Before I could talk to you about a creative God, I would have to define what I mean when I say "God." And before I could define God, I would have to talk about the limitations of language.

It is not intellectually honest to use undefined words and give pat answers. It is almost as silly as walking into a large factory, pointing to a piece of machinery that is hooked up to an entire assembly line and asking about the function of a sole, tiny screw. I first would have to explain how the piece of machinery plugs into the assembly line, what the assembly line produces, and the mission and the purpose of the factory. Only then would you understand and appreciate that screw.

This is what has happened to our generation of Jews. Many of us don't know much Torah, and what we do know are bits and pieces out of context. When we get involved in discussions about whether the Torah is true or not, we have no idea—or the wrong idea—of what it is in the first place. If we have the wrong idea, we are at best looking at a partial picture, or worse yet, a distorted picture of what it is—of what Judaism is.

It is my aim in this book to bring into focus many distorted pictures and in so doing offer uncommon answers to common questions that people ask about Jewish identity, faith, and daily Jewish practices. Although any chapter can be read on its own, I strongly discourage that. The process of presentation here will be similar to watching a photo develop. Never does a picture develop from the top down or the bottom up. A little gray appears in one corner; a little dark appears in another. The picture could be very misleading during the developing process, but when it is finished, there it finally appears—a complete picture, crisp and clear and in full focus.

A hint of this concept is found in the Hebrew word for truth, *emet*. The word *emet*—spelled *aleph, mem, tav*—spans the entire Hebrew alphabet. The first letter is *aleph*, the last letter is *tav*, and the middle letter is *mem*, hinting to us that truth goes from the beginning to the end and includes the entire middle.

Because of its wholeness, it is very difficult to know where to start when talking about truth. You will understand the material at the beginning much more by the time you get to the end. In fact, the more you read the chapters, the more the ideas will start to make sense, and you will begin to see the larger picture.

Keeping this in mind, we can begin.

1.

Unpacking Your Spiritual Baggage

I ONCE WAS HIRED to organize educational programs for a large Jewish youth group in the United States. To overcome any possible stigmas associated with the word *rabbi* and to encourage the kids to relate to me without preconceived notions, I asked the executives to introduce me simply as David Aaron, not as Rabbi David Aaron. They respected my request, but I was dismayed to read in their newsletter the following announcement: "We want to welcome a new member to our staff: David Aaron, our Judaism specialist."

This sounded even worse! It implied that Judaism was some sort of disease; after all, don't you go to a *specialist* when you have a disease your general practitioner can't treat? When do you go to a Judaism specialist? When you suffer from Jewish guilt? I was in trouble even before I started.

I had wanted to be just another person on the staff. I didn't want my name to have anything Jewish, Hebrew, or rabbinic attached to it, because I knew that any overt identification with Judaism would immediately connect me in the kids' minds to whatever Jewish baggage they carried. It turned out I was right. And, needless to say, I had a rough time, but this was the beginning of essential lessons I needed to learn.

Twenty-two years in the field of education have taught me how to help people unpack their spiritual baggage. The first step is to unlock the suitcase and look at what's inside. This process involves examining what you think you already know about Judaism and your issues with it. If you want to take a spiritual journey, you'll have to unpack the bags you've been carrying from a long guilt trip.

It's hard for people to imagine just how much Jewish baggage they really have, and to see that various past experiences, images, and definitions are actually stifling their ability to really understand the true meaning of their heritage. To unpack this baggage is the first step to spiritual growth.

For example, most people are unaware of the images that naturally surface in their minds when they hear the word *God*, and they often do not realize just how oppressive those images can be. The same goes for the words *commandment* and *Torah*, as well as many other words related to Judaism. They are unaware of the biased images that are stored in their heads, and when these images surface, they assume that what comes to mind is true.

Such personal biases are the first stumbling block to spiritual growth. If you really want to grow, then you must get in touch with what you think you already know, and you must be willing to ask yourself whether your perceptions reflect reality.

NEGATIVE IMAGES

Although we may consider ourselves broad minded and well informed, all too often our perceptions are based on a narrow range of encounters and limited experiences. Once we have an experience, we define it and categorize it. And once we've categorized an experience, our definition of it becomes an unconscious absolute that we may need to work hard to get beyond.

This is true for many Jewish adults when it comes to God, Judaism, Israel, and Torah. They have formulated their definitions and stored them (alongside other negative images in their heads) and they don't realize just how deeply engraved these images are, and just how much these images are stifling their ability to feel pride in their tradition.

To illustrate this point, I've often asked people to describe their image of a Torah sage or holy person. Most people imagine a frail old man with a long beard, often wearing thick glasses. Why can't it be a young man or a woman? There are young men and women who are Torah sages. But when most people imagine "Torah sage," they think of a frail old man. Is this an attractive—or real—image?

When I was growing up, I had a very clear image of a Torah sage; it came from a picture in my parents' living room that depicted three very old rabbis with long white beards and glasses. They were sitting bent over around a table piled with books, seemingly engaged in a Talmudic argument. One looked like an umpire yelling, "You're out!" The other one looked like he was shouting, "No!" And the third one seemed to be mouthing, "Oy Vey!"

To me, that picture was Judaism. I did not like it, I could not relate to it, and I did not want to see myself in it. I did not want to be weak and old. I did not want to be sitting in that dark gloomy room, bent over a pile of books, involved in some irrelevant Talmudic debate. That unattractive picture was my baggage.

Later in life, I realized that this picture, which my parents had bought in Israel, had actually determined for me what a Torah sage looked like. For a long time that picture was my only image of Judaism, because it was engraved in my mind—a graven image, so to speak. And I had to work hard to get past it.

I was confronted with the falsity of that image when I finally met a real Torah sage. I had a very personal question that I needed help with and decided I must ask a master of the Kabbalah, who would know the secrets of the Torah because Kabbalah is the deepest understanding of the Torah. So I asked around whom it would be best to consult. That is how I found out about a great Kabbalah master, a Hassidic rebbe called the Z'viler Rebbe. I had never heard of him and did not know where to find him. But I figured that he must live in Meah Shearim, the famous Hassidic neighborhood in Jerusalem. Where else could he be?

I went to Meah Shearim and started asking where to find the Rebbe from Z'vil. The first person I asked knew precisely, gave me a set of complex directions, and of course I got lost.

I then met someone else on the street and said, "Excuse me, have you heard of the Z'viler Rebbe?" "Have I heard of the Z'viler Rebbe? Oy gevalt, he's such a holy man, an unbelievably deep soul."

This time I managed to keep the directions straight. When

I got to the right place, I saw a young fellow walking up the stairs and I asked once more for the home of the Z'viler Rebbe." He said, "I can take you there."

"Great."

As we were walking up the stairs I asked this young guy, "Have you ever met this Rebbe?"

He said, "You might say so, yes." He got to the door and said, "This is where the Z'viler Rebbe lives."

He took the keys out of his pocket, and I said, "You work for the Z'viler Rebbe?" But he must not have heard me, because he opened the door and directed me to a room in the back of the house. While I was waiting there, all kinds of images and fantasies were flying because a Hassidic master was about to walk in, full of fire, and it was going to be like lightning!

After a while, this same young fellow walked into the room, sat across the desk and said, "How can I help you?"

Puzzled, I said again, "I'm looking for the Z'viler Rebbe."

"I'm the Z'viler Rebbe."

You can imagine my utter shock.

I had completely the wrong idea of what a great Kabbalah master *must* look like. Surely he had to be old. He had to be intimidating. I had trembled at the thought of even asking my question, and had the issue not been so pressing, I might have never searched for him—I would have been too afraid.

FALSE PERCEPTIONS

Once I corrected my image of a Torah sage, I had to correct my idea of what to expect from a Torah sage.

When I was in my 20s, I entered a yeshiva to get my rabbinical ordination. After several years, I felt that I would like to leave full-time learning and start teaching. Because there are so many Jews in the world that know so little about Judaism, I wanted to share what I had learned thus far. But I wasn't sure if it was the right thing to do just then—perhaps it was too early, perhaps I was not learned enough. I decided to ask a Torah scholar, Rabbi Joseph Shalom Eliyashiv, for advice. Rabbi Eliyashiv is considered to be one of the greatest Torah authorities of our generation, and I was a little nervous to meet him. I shared with him my dilemma and asked him, "What does God want me to do?"

Rabbi Eliyashiv turned to me and said, "You have no responsibility right now to go out to the community. You are still young. Therefore, you should continue to sit and learn." Hearing that, I must have made a very contorted face, because he asked, "What's wrong?"

Spontaneously I said, "But I'm not happy sitting and learning anymore. I want to go out and teach!"

"Why, then, are you asking questions?" he demanded.

"I beg your pardon," I stammered.

"Why are you asking questions?"

"Because I want to know, what is it that God wants me to do?"

"God wants you to be happy, of course! You didn't tell me in the beginning that you weren't happy in the yeshiva."

Because of my baggage, I did not realize that I could tell a great rabbi that I wasn't happy. I did not think that it was important. In fact, I thought the more you suffer the holier you must be. This was the first time I had heard any rabbi say, "God wants you to be happy." Can you imagine my surprise and relief? Had I not made that contorted face, and had Rabbi Eliyashiv not been sensitive enough to see it, I would have walked out of his office and sat in yeshiva for another 10 years, feeling miserable and thinking myself a holy martyr. It may sound crazy, but that was part of my baggage. I did not think that happiness was a consideration in Jewish law. But here was one of the greatest rabbis of our time saying, "Of course you should be happy. If you're not happy sitting and learning, and you'd be happier going out and teaching, then do it. Don't you think teaching Torah is important?"

I had never identified the word *happiness* with the word God. I had been stuck with a false image of Judaism and had not even realized it. I was trapped by my very narrow ideas, which got in the way of my ability to enjoy being Jewish.

Many Jews are in a similar position, and the usual reason they can't connect with Judaism is a negative image from their childhoods—and some of these people were brought up in religious homes!

NEGATIVE AND POSITIVE IDENTIFICATION

I have met people from religious backgrounds who once kept Shabbat, ate kosher, and prayed three times a day. But these practices were joyless and came with a lot of fear, oppression, and guilt. These people's negative experiences turned into painful triggers that, ultimately, forced them to run from God and any religious institution.

How the mind stores images and then reacts to triggers is an amazing psychological phenomenon. Most of us have had the experience of, for example, driving a car and, all of a sudden, feeling overcome by a sad feeling. We get in a bad mood—though we are doing nothing, just driving—and we don't know why.

The word psychologists use to describe this phenomenon is *identification*. What can happen is this:

While you are driving you hear a song on the radio that happened to be playing in a restaurant when you were breaking up with your boyfriend or girlfriend ten years ago. You may not have known that the song was playing at the time; it could have been background music. As you were experiencing that traumatic moment, this song was playing, "She loves you, yeah, yeah, yeah," and you did not even notice it. Then one day you happen to be feeling really happy. You are driving down the highway, it's a beautiful day, and the radio announcer says, "Now let's hear a song from the Beatles." "She loves you, yeah, yeah, yeah." You're just listening, and all of a sudden you're getting very depressed. You don't know why you're feeling depressed, but the words "She loves you, yeah, yeah, yeah" access that feeling in your memory bank.

This same kind of reaction is triggered in many of us regarding Judaism. And when that happens, our minds bring up a lot of baggage.

I once heard that some circus trainers teach bears to dance by making them walk on hot coals. When the bear is forced to walk on hot coals, it makes jagged movements from the pain.

As the bear is walking over the coals and shaking in pain, the trainer plays music that later becomes a trigger for the bear. So, when the music starts to play and the circus brings out the dancing bear for all to watch with wonder and joy, in fact, the bear's heart cries because he is in a lot of pain. A similar thing happens for many people when it comes to religion.

I don't think most of us have such intense feelings of repulsion towards Jewish tradition, but nonetheless, we need to be sure to unpack our baggage, get off our guilt trip, and start on a healthy spiritual journey.

At Isralight, the organization I founded and run internationally, we once had an ad campaign with a slogan that read in big print: "Want to love it?" Then, in smaller print, the ad continued: "Many Jews simply don't love being Jewish. They may be proud of it, but does it excite their minds, warm their hearts, or spark their souls?" Within the first hour of putting the poster on the street, we received our first call. It was a man who said he would like to meet me and find out more about the program.

When he arrived in my office, I was shocked to find a religious Jew standing before me. He had the poster in his hand. "Who is this for?" he asked.

"What do you mean?" I was puzzled.

"Well," he continued, "I've been religious all my life, but when I read this poster I realized that I don't love it. Although I'm living it, I'm not loving it. Is this program for someone like me?"

I had originally founded my organization for people who had little, if any, knowledge of Judaism. But this fellow was very advanced in terms of knowing Jewish law, and he was also committed to Jewish practice, yet the soul of his practice was missing. This fellow did not love it. It was then that I realized that I wanted Isralight to be also for someone like him, because everyone deserves to know the true meaning and joy of living Jewish.

So this man joined Isralight, learning alongside other people who had very little background in Jewish studies. It is quite remarkable that a person like him could be involved in Judaism and not really love it, not really enjoy it. Many people don't believe they could or even should enjoy and love it. But you can.

Not only can you love being Jewish, when you truly understand it, you'll wonder how you could have ever not loved it. And you will want to celebrate it daily.

2.

What's in It for Me?

PEOPLE IN THE advertising business know that to sell any product the ad has to answer the question "What's in it for me?" because that is the foremost question, albeit subconscious, in the mind of any consumer. When it comes to exploring Judaism, "What's in it for me?" may not be a common question that people *explicitly* ask, but it is *the* question that is very much on their minds—whether they are aware of it or not.

People often don't even begin to explore Judaism because it is already clear to them that the answer to "What's in it for me?" is a restrictive life of archaic religious dogma based on blind faith.

I once received a letter from a woman who wanted to participate in a seminar at Isralight. The letter read:

Dear Rabbi,

I've been living with a non-Jew for five years. We were engaged, and about a month before the wedding I decided I couldn't marry him. When he asked me why, I said, "Because you're not Jewish." He said, "Betty, we've been living together for five years and we love each other. Plus, you've always confided in me that you dislike Jews." It was true, I do dislike Jews, but I could not marry him, because he was not Jewish.

So Rabbi, I broke up with a man I love for an identity that I don't love, and I don't know why. So do you think that this program would be for me?

Of course I welcomed Betty, but though she enrolled, she did not show up. When I finally met her later, she apologized and offered this explanation: "I decided not to participate, because I realized that I'm not a . . . er . . . *religious* personality."

"What does that have to do with it?" I asked her. "If I remember correctly, I got this letter from you, and you were living with a man for five years and then decided to break it off because he was not Jewish."

"Oh, that," she sighed. "I figured it out for myself. I couldn't marry Tony, because I'm a granddaughter of a rabbi!"

"And you fear your grandfather's disapproval?"

"No, he's dead. He died in the Holocaust."

"I don't understand."

"I can't marry a non-Jew," she said, "because my grandfather died as a Jew."

"Betty," I said, "do you think that your grandfather died for some stupid dogma?"

"Rabbi, that's exactly what I don't want you to confirm."

And that was her problem. She was so convinced that Judaism was a stupid religion, that Judaism had very little to offer an intellectual personality or a spiritual personality. When I asked her why she thought Judaism was so stupid, she started spewing out many untruths. I could understand where she got her information, because I knew that many others believe what she did about Judaism. But it was not really Judaism—it was a totally false image of what Judaism is.

Betty did not consider herself a religious personality, but she was religiously running away from religion. In fact, her blind belief that she knew what it was—and that it was stupid—didn't let her see what Judaism had to offer her.

FROM THE OY TO THE JOY

The word *religion* has a stigma. For some people, it's a dirty word. In some way, the notion of a religious person conjures up an image of someone who is a loser, who needs a crutch and therefore runs away from the real world seeking the protective womb of religion and shelter from life's challenges. Happy confident people who are powerful and successful in the real world don't need religion.

This stereotyping has historical roots. Most people remember what Karl Marx said, "Religion is the opiate of the masses." Some may also be familiar with Nietzsche's theory. He described two types of people in the world, strong and weak. Strong people do what they want, when they want, and where they want. Weak people don't; generally they are subjugated by the strong. To outsmart the strong, weak people invented "morality" in order to make the strong feel guilty about doing whatever they wanted to whomever they wanted. These "smart weak people," Nietzsche said, were the Jews, and the Christians who adopted their ideas and foisted them onto the rest of humankind. Nietzsche's ideas have permeated much of Western thinking, and today many of us believe that religion is a plot to make people feel guilty about what they want to do and enjoy doing. Religion robs us of our confidence and strength to assert ourselves. Religion forbids everything that is fun and pleasurable in life. Religion has turned humanity into a bunch of wimps servile to some almighty, supernatural dictator.

For those who look at Judaism this way their answer to the question "What's in it for me?" is "Nothing but trouble."

Despite attempts to discredit the stature of religious believers in general, Judaism is really about gaining the wisdom and empowerment to maximize the quality of your life and fully celebrate each day, specifically by reclaiming your inner godly self and connecting with the source of all life—God.

Judaism clarifies the essential beliefs that inspire and enable us to live a purposeful, passionate, and pleasurable life soaring to the greatest heights of vitality, meaning, and joy.

BELIEFS THAT MAKE OR BREAK US

To believe or not to believe: that is *not* the question. Everybody believes in something. It might not be Judaism or one of the popular religions, but there is nobody in the world who doesn't have a set of beliefs regarding human nature, life, and the beyond. Even those people who maintain that there is nothing beyond life, or that life is meaningless, are subscribing to a particular belief. And they, just as much as fervent believers in God, are compelled by their beliefs and act on their beliefs whether or not they are aware of it.

Religion—when defined as a set of beliefs—doesn't necessarily have to include God. Indeed, some people are religious "hockey players." The sport is a ritual that requires certain uniforms, specific times and settings, and various exercises. It creates a community and it gives the players a high. And it is based on a belief that at least part of life was meant for fun and games. Some people may not like to term this religion, because God is absent from it. But when you really think about it, in a general sense, religion is simply a set of beliefs and a lifestyle derivative of those beliefs.

Furthermore, everyone already has certain legalistic or ritualistic norms of behavior, commanded primarily by his or her set of beliefs.

For instance, let's say you believe that we are just animals, this is a dog-eat-dog world, life is just a fleeting moment, and there is nothing lasting beyond the physical pleasures of this world. If that is truly what you believe, then that is exactly the way you will live your life. You will act like an aggressive animal, ruthlessly going after what you want regardless of all the other human dogs you will have to bite to get it. You will grab what you can while you can, cramming as much pleasure as possible into every moment. And you couldn't care less about any future ramifications of your behavior.

What you believe determines what you do and who you become. Your beliefs can either empower you or destroy you. Your beliefs could lead you to tremendous excellence in your life and enable you to build an incredible world for yourself and others, or your beliefs can destroy you and the world.

Therefore, embracing beliefs that are empowering and invig-
orating is the most important thing you can do to guarantee
yourself the best life possible. Your beliefs are the foundation
of everything in your life.

Belief in God is a person's most powerful belief and yet po-
tentially also the most dangerous belief. Belief in God has empowered people to do amazing things, but it has also influenced
people to do horrible crimes. The most beautiful things and the
most destructive things have been done in the name of God.
The kind of God you believe in can determine if your life will
be creative or destructive, joyful or miserable.

Tony Robbins, the famous self-improvement expert and lec-
turer, describes a psychology concept called neuro-linguistic
programming (NLP), which is appropriate to understanding
the powerful role of beliefs in our lives. In his book *Unlimited
Power*, he says "beliefs help us tap the richest resources deep
within us, creating and directing these resources in the support
of our desired outcomes. Beliefs are the compass and maps that
guide us toward our goals and give us the surety to know that
we'll get there. Without beliefs or the ability to tap into them,
people can be totally disempowered. They are like a motorboat
without a motor or rudder. With powerful guiding beliefs, you
have the power to take action and create the world that you
want to live in."[1]

NLP actually subscribes to a basic principle of Judaism, modeling. In essence, if you model yourself after another person, you
can achieve what he or she has achieved. The first things you
have to do when modeling another person are clarify his or her

beliefs and follow them. Only after you embrace the person's beliefs will you be able to model his or her accomplishments.

Judaism is founded on this very principle—emulating God, or modeling oneself according to what God believes about humans, life, and the beyond. According to Judaism, we are partners with God in creating the world. With the powerful guiding beliefs that form the Jewish religion, you have the ability to create the best possible world, one that is informed by the ideals and values of God.

Judaism doesn't need confirmation from Tony Robbins, but I think it is important for people who are learning about Judaism to see the correlation between Judaism and modern psychology. In no way am I suggesting that modern ideas are proofs or support for Judaism's ancient beliefs. They are simply interesting correlations. The point is this: there is no more powerful directing force in your behavior than your beliefs. To take control of your life, you must have clarity about your beliefs, because it is your beliefs that command your actions, inform your lifestyle, and determine the quality of your life.

So what *do* you really believe? This is one of the most important questions you will have to ask yourself to succeed in really living life to its max.

Here's an exercise to help you get started. Write down three beliefs that you have about humanity, life, and the beyond. Once you've articulated your beliefs, arrange them in order of how much each belief guides your life and moves you. Next, look at your set of beliefs and write down how they influence your behavior in specific ways.

Such exercises can help you appreciate the relationship between Torah and its commandments. The Torah is not simply a book of interesting philosophical or mystical concepts. Torah is a set of beliefs regarding the nature of reality—humanity, life, and the beyond. Every belief engenders an innate ethos that directs and guides our behavior. Every commandment flows naturally from a certain Torah belief regarding the nature of reality. Judaism claims that these principles of belief express what God believes and how God acts. And when we model ourselves after God we too become like God. So the answer to "What's in it for me?" is the power to become like God, to become the ultimate incredible godly you.

ACTION SPEAKS

At this point you are probably wondering, "If this is true, why are there people who espouse the beliefs of Judaism and yet don't seem so enlightened, empowered, or happy? Sometimes, even though people say they believe, their behavior may say something completely different."

I have met people who were raised in religious homes where they were taught to believe in God, yet later in life they became atheists. I also have met people from atheist homes where their parents taught them that there is no God, yet now they are profoundly involved with God. How it is possible that a person raised one way can turn out another way?

This is a very important point: people's actions speak louder and clearer than what they say in words. A parent can't say, "Don't do what I do, do what I say!" Our most direct and revealing communication is our behavior. Therefore our children learn from watching our behavior and the behavior of others. But sometimes we are not in touch with what we really believe. We may know what we want to believe or are supposed to believe, and we may know the right answers because we are taught to give the right answers.

However, despite our programming, our behavior will always reveal what we really believe. If you grew up in an environment where your parents preached belief in God yet they treated people like dirt, then what they *really* taught you is that there is no God. In essence, they told you that this world is an accident and there is no value to human life, because there is no difference between a human being and a piece of dirt. People who believe that human beings are created in God's image do not treat people like dirt.

I also have seen parents who say they don't believe in God, yet they treat every human being as if they are created in the image of God, leaving their children with the profound feeling that life couldn't simply be an accident. So it's important to understand that people can live an absolute contradiction in their lives, whereby their behavior does not reflect what they profess to be their beliefs. These people are simply lying to themselves.

Dating is fertile ground for seeing these contradictions. Conversations can go very well, with both people envisioning the same ideals, yet one person's behavior may have nothing to do with these ideals. These people may talk about what they would like to believe, while their behavior reveals what they actually believe. For dating to lead to a successful marriage, two people must have clarity about each other's beliefs by seeing whether they actually express their beliefs through consistent action.

Judaism not only offers clear and empowering general principles of belief, it also gives us a very detailed way of behaving and interacting that puts those beliefs into our everyday actions.

I have, unfortunately, met seemingly religious Jews whose behavior went against their acclaimed beliefs. But if they truly abided by the principles of Judaism and its rules of behavior, they would not act in such inappropriate ways, or they would at least struggle to change and integrate with what they *say* they believe. In my experience, these people are exceptions to the rule, so please do not allow them to confuse your understanding of Judaism. You cannot judge a book by its cover; so too, you cannot always judge a religion by some of its self-acclaimed advocates.

In general, we see throughout history what Jewish belief and its daily lifestyle accomplished for the Jewish people. There is a high moral conscience and spiritual aura prevalent in Torah-abiding communities. And the absolute miracle of Jewish survival against all odds is also a remarkable testimony to the power of Jewish belief to rise above the most trying and painful situations.

SEEING THROUGH BLIND FAITH

Getting in touch with the source of your beliefs can open your eyes to those things that you accept without question.

Your parents were your first stop. They created you and your world, guided your actions, and set up certain life principles for you. They formed your first image of God because they were your first "gods." It may be that you are still struggling with this image and its negative effect upon you.

Your education, your environment, society, the media—all impact what you believe, whether you realize it or not. Even people who are other than your immediate family, whether or not you chose them as role models, have influenced you, sometimes positively and sometimes negatively. You've picked up influences on the street, at work, in your home, and from movies.

To paint a clearer picture for yourself, try to pinpoint one belief that you got from your parents, from either what they said or what they did. Think about a certain rule that your parents held or certain statements they often made. What comes to my mind when I do this exercise is "Eat your dinner and don't let it go to waste. There are children starving in Biafra." What I could not understand as a child was why we couldn't just send it to them if I didn't want to eat it. "Hang up your coat" was another repeated theme in my house. In fact, when I think of it, I realize that I still forget to hang up my coat. Funny, this is now what I have to say to my kids. Until they see me hang up my coat, they're not going to hang up their coats.

Once you start delving into the origins of your beliefs, you'll start to realize how much society and peer pressure have influenced you, even in the most silly and superficial ways. Here's a prime example: A boy should never button his top shirt button. All through grade school, if a boy buttoned his top button, then he was a nerd, a real loser. I remember a boy named Lenny, who always came to school with his top button closed, at the expense of having no friends. No one in the entire fourth grade talked to poor Lenny.

The media also has a huge influence on our beliefs. For example, for some people it's an unwritten law that "things go better with Coke." We don't realize that when we walk into a store and we're thirsty that this advertisement starts dictating what drink we're going to choose. If we hear over and over again that things go better with Coke, then we are likely to buy a Coke. But then again, if we want to feel cool and hip and show our defiance, we might choose 7-Up, "the Uncola."

Getting in touch with the origins of your beliefs—your parents, your peers, and society—will help you understand just how much you have been influenced. Once you realize this fact, you'll have a greater ability to clarify your beliefs and the impact they are having on your actions and your relationships. Realize that your beliefs, whether you are aware of them or not, are your personal religion. If you want to take control of your life, then you need to know what you really believe and how it affects the quality of your life and your relationships. And then you can ask yourself: Is this what I want to believe and is this the way I want to be and behave? Do these beliefs correlate to what life, love, success, and so on are really all about? Are these beliefs empowering or disempowering?

In essence all of us are already religious, even those of us who have never gone to synagogue or church, even those of us who have never before picked up a book about religion. We all adhere to principles in which we believe. But many of us rarely know why we believe what we believe, where our beliefs come from, and whether or not our beliefs have been proven to be true. Yet these beliefs are directing our behavior, affecting our relationships, and determining the quality of our lives.

Every one of us follows a certain set of laws, whether we are aware of it or not. Even those of us who are against accepting the rigor of Jewish law also live according to many laws. Simply, we have rules. Brush your teeth in the morning: that's a rule. We do it and it's natural, so we would not consider it a law. It's not like we get up in the morning and think, "Now I have to serve God, and if I don't brush my teeth, then my teeth are not going to make it into the world to come." We abide by a systematic behavioral pattern, whether we know it or not. Generally, we don't know it, and thus we're not in control of our lives.

It is important to understand that many of the people who accuse religious people of being dogmatic and having blind faith also base their lives on personal dogma and on blind faith. Unless they know the answer to the question "Where did I get this belief and how do I know that it is true?" they are basing their lives on dogma and blind faith.

Questioning our beliefs is vital to growing up and taking responsibility. When we are children we create a map of how to get from point A to point B. Children raised in an abusive home will come to believe certain things about themselves and life, and as a result of these beliefs, they will formulate certain rules about how to survive. They may conclude that the first commandment to survive in this mean world is "Thou shalt lie." As they mature and meet up with different settings, people, and challenges, they will have to question whether the beliefs they adopted as children represent reality in the adult world.

The difficulty as we grow up is to clarify what we really believe. Sometimes we need to say to a friend, "Tell me, you've seen my behavior, you've seen the way I interact with people. What would you think I believe?" We can start to determine how much we really believe in something according to how the belief has influenced our behavior and whether or not we've created a behavioral pattern that reinforces the belief.

GET A LIFE

Once we start to question our beliefs, our real search for truth begins. Truth is a set of beliefs that correlates to reality. It is when your map (your beliefs) reflects the terrain (reality).

Imagine your frustration if you are in Italy looking for a local map and someone hands you a map of Jerusalem. For some reason, you don't notice that it says *Jerusalem* at the top. As you consult the map for the nearest public bathroom, you follow this line and that line, go left here and right there. Sure enough, where you think the public bathroom should be located, you see a fountain with a cupid urinating into a pond. You say, "My gosh! Is this the way they do it in Italy?"

Essentially, you are frustrated because you realize that your set of beliefs does not correlate with reality. In the same way, if the map that guides your approach to life is drawn according to the belief that it is a dog-eat-dog world, then you're going to view everyone around you as if he or she is a dog who is out to get you. Your attitude will tremendously affect how you see the world. You will interpret everything according to your set of beliefs. But what if your beliefs are not true? What if the world really is not full of vicious dogs?

When Judaism claims that its basic beliefs are true, it means that they correlate with the way reality truly is. In order to influence our behavior and thought in accordance with truth, or reality, Judaism outlines 613 commandments for us to follow. Nowadays we're not obligated to follow all 613, because many of these commandments relate to the service in the Temple and no longer apply because the Temple was destroyed by the Romans in 70 CE. But it is important to understand the real meaning of these commandments and how they benefit our lives. They are not just random acts that God wants us to do. The commandments put us in sync with what life is really all about. The commandments embody beliefs that correlate to what truly is.

Remember, the search for truth is to find the set of beliefs and a lifestyle that are correlative and congruent with the terrain of life. The door prize for living the commandments is feeling in touch with reality, experiencing the joy of living in concert with what is real.

Halacha, Jewish law, is Judaism's map. The word *halacha*

literally means "path," or "walkway." It's much deeper than law. A walkway helps you to get from point A to point B. It's a directive based on the understanding of the kind of mountains, rivers, and valleys that make up the terrain of our life, whether the journey is spiritual, physical, psychological, or sociological. The terrain is full of peaks and valleys that we need to traverse to reach our destination. To succeed in our journey we need a map, a set of beliefs, and the correlative acts that reflect the terrain of reality.

The word G-O-D is not written in the Torah. When the original Hebrew text was translated, someone decided to use that word. However, the Hebrew word that refers to the divine is the unpronounceable Tetragrammaton YHVH. It is the derivative of the Hebrew words for "was," "is," and "will be." YHVH suggests the ever present, the source, context, ground, and essence of all being, the ultimate timeless reality. Judaism's principles of belief, commandments, and laws are meant to enable us to live conscious of and in concert with YHVH—ultimate timeless reality.

To find truth, you have to let go of any preconceived notions you may have when you hear the word God. Otherwise they will interfere with your ability to understand the terrain of life, to understand what reality is—or "who reality is"—because reality is alive, conscious, and caring. We will discuss this in greater detail in the next chapter.

The Power to Portray, or Betray?

Thus far we have said that religion is really a set of beliefs regarding the nature of reality and our relationship to reality. Truth is a set of beliefs that correlates to and coordinates us with reality.

So where does faith fit in? Doesn't all this simply come down to faith?

In Judaism, there is no such thing. You may hear people use the word *faith* in reference to Judaism, but the term is inaccurate. In fact, we must be very careful to use accurate terminology because the journey of finding truth requires tremendous precision. So to be cautious, I want to stress that Judaism does not believe in faith. Once again, a Hebrew term has been loosely translated into English and its original meaning has become confused. *Emuna* is the original Hebrew term that is translated into English as the word *faith*. To understand the true definition of *emuna*, we have to examine its original meaning and its association with other similar Hebrew terms.

Interestingly, the word *emuna* is correlated to three Hebrew words. One is *ne'eman*, which means "faithful/dedicated." Another is *omanut*, which means "artistry." The third is *emunim*, meaning "exercises." Therefore, *emuna* suggests faithfulness, art, and exercise. In other words, *emuna* is a consistent exercise dedicated to faithfully portraying reality and our relationship to it as it truly is.

Think about what an artist does. For example, an artist has

the ability to paint love. If you were an artist and you wanted to paint love, what would you paint? A typical answer is a mother holding a child with an affectionate look on her face. It is possible to portray abstract ideas in very real terms. Judaism believes in this concept wholeheartedly.

To illustrate the point, imagine that you're walking down the street and you see someone give a poor man a dollar. You feel this action is right, that it is a portrayal of reality. Then you walk down the street and you see someone go up to a poor man and kick him. You feel this is wrong, that it is not truth, not congruent with reality. You have a sense that behavior can portray something real or not real.

Emuna is not expressed though statements of "I believe this and I believe that." *Emuna* is an exercise that we must do every single day of our life: to portray reality so that what we are saying in action is true and real and not a lie.

In English, the Hebrew word *chet* would be translated as "transgression" or "sin." However, according to Judaism, *chet* is really a betrayal of reality. Judaism teaches that the ultimate question in life is whether we will succeed in portraying reality or betraying reality. To portray reality and be in harmony with reality—in essence, at one with God—we live the commandments of the Torah. But a *chet* is a betrayal of reality—we act in a way that cuts us off from what is real. It is not only a betrayal of God but also a betrayal of ourselves because it removes us from our source, ground, and essence of life—God. We are simply living an illusion divorced from reality. The Talmud teaches that a person transgresses only if and when a spirit of insanity comes over him. Sane people—those who live in accordance with reality—don't transgress.

Judaism teaches that we innately know the truth. Our soul is a part of the ultimate reality. Therefore, when we are in touch with our soul, we fulfill the commandments naturally.

A verse in the Psalms of David explains the practical meaning of *emuna*: "All Your commandments are *emuna*."[2] At first glance, the line is difficult to understand. But if we apply what we know about the commandments—that they are acts that successfully express and portray reality and our relationship to it—we'll begin to understand.

Since *emuna* is faithfulness to reality, we can understand that our faithfulness is manifest by a lifestyle—a set of behaviors—that demonstrates what is real. The commandments demonstrate truth and they correlate us to reality. In other words, when we follow God's commandments, we're in sync with reality.

The bottom line is this: a person of faith is not a person who says, "I believe." It doesn't matter what a person says they believe; what matters is what a person does. According to Judaism, the way you say *I believe* is through your actions. It's by following the commandments in detail as outlined in *halacha*, Jewish law, which are actions that portray the truth.

Living a life of *emuna*—a life in which your beliefs and behaviors are harmonious with reality—requires you to go beyond simply asking yourself what you *should* do. Imagine that you got into the bad habit of kicking every poor person that you saw. People would tell you that you shouldn't do that; that you could go to prison because of it. After deciding that, indeed, you don't want to go to prison, you decide to work on changing your behavior. You then begin to realize that you should not be kicking old men. However, once you have kicked the habit of kicking, you come to realize that the change in you is not motivated by someone telling you that you *should not* do this. Rather, the change in you has happened because it is reality not to kick people and to do otherwise is to lose touch with reality and to lose touch with your inner godly essence.

Emuna means to live the truth not because of shoulds and should nots imposed upon you from without, but because of the compelling principles of the beliefs that come from within your soul as it connects to the ultimate reality—God.

IN SUMMARY

Let's recap what we've learned. Religion is a set of beliefs regarding humanity, life, and the beyond—the nature of reality and our relationship to it.

Truth is a set of beliefs that describes reality as it truly is. True beliefs put us in touch with reality.

Emuna is the power to take that truth, that set of beliefs, and translate it into actions that are real, actions that portray our inner self as part of the timeless ultimate reality—God.

We are all religious. We all have a set of beliefs about humanity, life, and the beyond. We all believe something about reality and our relationship to it. And we are all under the command of those beliefs—faithful to our beliefs and acting them out daily. However, does our daily lifestyle correlate to what we say we believe? And are our beliefs true? Do they correlate to reality and empower us to express and be who we really are?

Judaism puts us in touch with reality. It empowers us to become like God, to express our inner godliness and experience the joy of being our truly incredible selves.

3.

Who Is God?

I ONCE ASKED a group of people to get in touch with their childhood image of God, to try to remember their earliest memory of what the word *God* brought up. This was one response from a woman in the class:

"When I think of God in my childhood," she related, "what comes up is my mother yelling at me. I must have done something wrong, because she was running after me, screaming, 'You bad girl, God's going to punish you.' So I ran into the bathroom and locked the door. My mother then banged on the door and yelled, 'Come out of there, you bad girl! God's going to punish you!' So I responded, 'No! He's not! I'm in the bathroom and He can't get me here.' At this, my mother said, 'You silly kid, God is everywhere, even in the bathroom.'"

As the woman told her story to the group, she said that she thought it was a funny story. The story, however, was quite sad. As a child, this woman learned that God is everywhere and He is out to get you. You cannot hide even in the washroom.

A punishing God is the first association for many people who grew up wondering, "What did I do wrong? Why is this happening to me?" This is a very serious false image of God. The woman who told this story was not totally aware of her baggage. During her participation in the Isralight program, I noticed that she oscillated between believing fervently in God and denying the existence of God. Her psychological conflict made sense because she had a very unhealthy—and false— image of God. She would have been healthier if she had not believed in God at all, because the God she believed in was de-stroying her life.

Quite frankly, I don't believe in God. The word spelled G-O-D does nothing for me; in fact, it interferes with my true belief.

I am not alone. Jews don't believe in God. Indeed, the word God is not found in the Torah or the rest of the Hebrew Bible. Moses never heard of God nor heard from God.

The name in the Torah that has been translated as God or Lord is composed of the Hebrew letters yud, hey, vav, hey— YHVH. When we see that name, Jewish people do something very odd: We say something else. We do not pronounce that name. When we see that name, we say a completely different name, Adonai (which does in fact mean "Lord" or "Master").

How very strange to see a name and say something else. We do this because we need to remember that what we see cannot be said. It is a constant reminder to accept humbly the limita-tions of our conceptual minds when referring to YHVH.

The Kabbalah warns in the Zohar that we should not affix any name or letter to the divine, because even the sacred word YHVH is, at best, only a tiny hint of the one who is beyond these words, names, or concepts. Because of this, the common practice in the Jewish world is to say HaShem, which literally means "The Name," and which, of course, refers to YHVH.

The Jewish people are very careful not to pronounce even the substitute name *Adonai* for YHVH—other than during prayer or during Torah reading—because we don't want to get familiar or comfortable with any name for the divine. The divine is, in fact, beyond all names, all terms, all images. Even the term *divine* suffers the limitations of narrow definition. But when we say *HaShem*, "The Name," we remind ourselves that we don't have a complete understanding of divinity.

OBSTACLES TO UNDERSTANDING

When we try to understand who *HaShem* refers to, we face an inherent obstacle with our descriptive vocabulary.

In general, we describe things in terms of time and space and in comparison to other objects. For example, in terms of time and space, you could describe this book as "now and here." You also could describe it relative to other objects: "smaller than a breadbox, but bigger than a teacup." If you are describing a person, you could say, "Harry lived for seventy years and died three years ago. He lived in a town five miles away from here. He was more intelligent than the average person, but he was also less emotional than most people." We have described Harry in terms of time and space, and compared him to other people.

But these terms or comparisons cannot be used to understand *HaShem*, because *HaShem* is the creator of time, space, and all beings, and therefore transcends these categories. Although it is common to say that God is "eternal" and "infinite," these terms are actually incorrect. For most people, eternal means something that goes on and on in time. But *HaShem* is the *source* of time. And time cannot confine or define *HaShem*. Infinite means something that goes on and on in space. But *HaShem* is the source of space. And space cannot confine or define *HaShem*.

Because descriptive language is inherently relative, it can never be accurate when applied to *HaShem*. If I say a table is large or small, I am describing it in relationship to other tables. If I describe it as "a mahogany table," the listener's mind automatically calls up its image of wood, learned from contrasting mahogany with pine, oak, or other woods. *HaShem*, however, is the source and creator of everything and, therefore, cannot be compared to *anything*.

People are accustomed to thinking in terms of time, space, and comparisons, so they automatically conceive of God as the one and only almighty being, who has no body, is eternal in time, and is infinite in space. This image is not only wrong, it is downright destructive. It is this kind of confusion that contributes to the mistaken thinking that humanity and God are separate and in conflict. We end up concluding that, if God is infinite and we are finite, then we are opposites and mutually exclusive; similarly, if God is eternal and we are temporary, then we are opposites and mutually exclusive.

Another obstacle to properly understanding *HaShem* is the limitation inherent in the standard approach to accessing knowledge. When I attempt to know anything, I am the subject, and I seek to know the object.

However, we can never know *HaShem* through this approach, because *HaShem* is the source of all knowledge and all consciousness. Our very ability to think comes from *HaShem*, who is the source of all thinking. How can we think about the source of all thinking? How can our mind hope to comprehend the source and ground of all minds?

It is important to understand that generally when people seek God, the reason they don't find God is that they are trying to understand God as an object in their minds, like anyone or anything else. But *HaShem* is not like anyone or anything else. *HaShem* cannot become an object to think about in one's mind, because *HaShem* is really the source of all thinking and the subject of all minds.

YHVH: The Ultimate Reality

Who is the Torah referring to when it speaks of *HaShem*? What does "The Name"—YHVH—really mean?

YHVH is associated with the Hebrew word *havaya*, meaning "existence/reality," and is formed out of the Hebrew verb *l'hiyot*, "to be." It is a permutation of the acronym for *haya, hoveh, v'yihiyeh*, which literally means "was, is, and will be."

In short YHVH means reality. YHVH is the ever-present context, content, ground, essence, and source of time, space, and all being. YHVH is the ultimate timeless reality.

In order for you and me to exist, we have to be *in* existence. But YHVH is not *in* existence. In fact, it is more correct to say that *existence* is in YHVH. YHVH is the ultimate reality who simply was, is, and always will be.

You and I did not always exist. At some point in time, we

came into existence. But YHVH did not come into existence, because YHVH is the original reality.

If you believe in the Big Bang Theory—that there was a primordial explosion which created masses of hot whirling gases that eventually condensed into stars and planets—you still have to consider a couple of points: Where did all of this happen? Who is the reality that supported and facilitated this event? Everyone starts off with the self-evident assumption that there is reality. Then, we try to understand and describe what happened *in* reality. But *what* is reality? The answer is YHVH.

When I say that *HaShem* is reality, some people object that "reality" sounds too impersonal. "What happened to the personal God?" they ask.

HaShem is not impersonal. If reality—YHVH—is the context, ground, essence, and source of you and me, then *HaShem* couldn't be any less personal than we are. In fact, *HaShem* is infinitely more personal. Reality—YHVH—is conscious, alive, and loving.

As we discussed earlier, the principles of Judaism, including its beliefs and laws, are meant to enable us to live conscious of and in concert with reality. Judaism is all about putting us in touch with reality. Only when we are firmly grounded in and connected to *HaShem*, who is the context, ground, and essence of all of existence, can we become fully real.

YHVH: The Ever Present

The fact that the words *haya, hoveh, v'yihiyeh*, are combined into one word, *YHVH*, means that *HaShem* "was, is, and will be" *simultaneously*. From the perspective of *HaShem*, the past, present, and future are all now. To you and me, the past *was*—it already happened and is now just a memory. The future *will be*—it has not happened yet—so it is now just a dream. For you and me, only the present is real.

To *HaShem*, however, all of history is like a mural of thousands of scenes painted on a canvas: it is all viewed and experienced as now. You and I are like ants walking across this canvas: we can see only small parts of the mural at a time. We remember the scenes that we have passed as the past. The scenes that we have not yet reached are the future. Then there is the scene where we are right now; we are present only in the present.

But *HaShem* is ever present—the past is now and the future is now. Appreciating this concept is the key to understanding prophecy. According to Judaism, Moses connected with *HaShem* and was therefore able to grasp the divine wisdom of the Torah and relate it to others. Coming from *HaShem*, the guidance embodied in the Torah's commandments is based on a complete picture of all of history, all stages of human development, all of time.

To connect to *HaShem*, who is fully present, we too must learn to be fully present in the now and conscious of the now. Our memories of the past and dreams for the future should not distract us from what we are doing in the present. They should not become worries and anxieties that destroy us and remove us from the now. Our ability to remember and to anticipate should be used only to help us think, speak, and act in the moment. Only the now is real, and only in the now can we connect to *HaShem*, the ever present.

Relating to YHVH

Judaism uses many other names to refer to the many aspects of YHVH: *Elohim, Shaddai, El*, to name a few. Each name suggests a different kind of relationship we have with *HaShem*. As with people, there is more than one kind of relationship we can have with *HaShem*.

I, too, have many names. My children call me Daddy, my students call me Rabbi, my parents call me Son. Each name indicates a unique kind of relationship with the one and only me, David.

So, when the Torah uses different divine names, it is indicating that there are different kinds of relationships to the divine, and, therefore, different perspectives on the one YHVH.

Let's say I have a discussion with my boss:

"JB, I would like to take my vacation next month."

"No!" JB emphatically says.

"But JB, I haven't taken any days off this year."

"No!" JB says again.

Then I say, "But come on, Dad . . . please?"

"Well, okay, son."

If JB is actually my boss and my father, then when I am in

the office I might call him JB, but at those times when I need to draw upon a deeper relationship, I call him Dad. So too, each divine name indicates a different kind of relationship with YHVH.

Despite the various divine names and their meanings, the only name that Judaism considers the essential one is the name YHVH. This name refers to the foundation of all other relations. My essential name is David. Even though some people call me Rabbi, Daddy, and so forth, it is David who is the rabbi and it is David who is the daddy. There are many types of relationships with and perspectives of the one and only David. The name YHVH expresses the basic relationship at the core of all other relationships.

And what is that relationship?

The Midrash, which is part of Jewish oral tradition, relates an interesting dialogue between Moses and *HaShem*. Moses asks *HaShem*, "What is your name?" *HaShem* responds, "According to my actions I am called." In other words, *HaShem* is saying, all the divine names that I am going to reveal to you correlate with what I do.

We can explain this Midrash with an analogy. If we saw someone singing, we would call her a singer. "Singer" is not her name, but it is a name that correlates to her particular action. If we saw someone dancing, we would call him a dancer. If we heard someone speaking, we would refer to her as the speaker. All these titles correlate to actions. In this same way, all the divine names correlate to actions of *HaShem* as we understand them.

The essential name, YHVH, correlates to the essential divine action, the act of being. Since the name *YHVH* is derived from the Hebrew word *li'hiyot*, "to be," perhaps the best translation of the YHVH would be "Be-er." (If you are speaking, then you are a speak-er. If you are writing, then you are a writer. And if you are being, then you are a be-er.)

After all, what does *to be* mean? Let's say that Joe is intelligent, and when we watch his actions, we can observe Joe *being* intelligent (i.e., expressing and manifesting his intelligence). So too with the universe, which is an expression and manifestation of *YHVH*. The entire universe is in the process of "being," a verb. If this is so, who then is the *noun*, the subject? It is the "Be-er."

When I realized that "Be-er" would be the best English translation of *YHVH*, I looked into a dictionary to see if there was such a word. Indeed, I found it in the Oxford Unabridged English Dictionary, along with this definition: "Be-er: One who is; the Self-existent, the great *I Am*."

Yes, YHVH is the Be-er, the source and subject of all being. And we are human *beings*.

This name for humanity reveals to us the amazing truth about ourselves: we, too, are verbs.

We are not the One Who Is. We are not the self-existent. And we are not the subject of all being, the great I Am. But if *HaShem* is the Be-er, then we are the manifestation of His being—we are human beings.

If *HaShem* were a painter, then we would be His painting. Indeed, all genuine artists have experienced a higher source of their creativity, whether or not they identified this source as divine. The sense of being a channel for a creative force that flows through you is an experience of *HaShem* as the subject.

Sometimes I write songs. Once I was sitting at my piano and started to play a beautiful song I had never heard before. I actually felt possessed; my fingers were moving without my telling them where to go. My wife walked into the room and asked, "What is this song?"

"I don't know," I replied. "I'm just trying to stay out of the way."

In such creative acts, the artist experiences that the painting or the poem or the dance is coming *through* him or her, not *from* him or her. The true source is somehow beyond the artist. This is an intuitive experience of *HaShem* as the source. In such moments of illumination we know *HaShem* as the Be-er, the source and subject of all being. We realize that we are beings/verbs.

Relating as verbs to *HaShem*, the subject, is the true meaning behind all the commandments. The commandments are like cables that connect us with our source. When the Jewish people received the Torah at Mt. Sinai, the first revelation they heard was really the compelling reason they would gladly want to perform *HaShem's* will.

The very first of the Ten Commandments requires us to know that "*I am* the Lord, your God, Who took you out of Egypt."[1]

This, of course, is not the only way to translate the original Hebrew text. It could also be translated, "The *I Am* is the Lord, your God, Who took you out of Egypt." This second translation describes the Jewish people as having the experience of the great *I Am*, the one and only subject, YHVH. By fulfilling the commandments, we connect with the great *I Am* and access the source of all being and creativity. This means that serving God is actually *self*-serving because God is the source of all self.

Therefore, according to Judaism, *HaShem* is not only the ultimate, ever-present reality, but also the ultimate *noun* and the source of all being. I'm a being and you're a being. There are all types of beings: physical beings, spiritual beings, mineral beings, vegetable beings, animal beings. But we're all verbs. Who then is the noun and the source of this great verb, *being*? The one whom we yearn to be conscious of and feel connected to.

The source of all being is the one I believe in and call YHVH—my Be-er. I don't believe in a God, a force, or spirit floating in outer space. *In* existence, there is no God. But YHVH *is* existence. YHVH *is* reality, and all of creation exists as a divine verb, an act of revelation and manifestation of *HaShem*.

The Ultimate Energy Source

The Kabbalah metaphorically describes all of existence as the endless light of *HaShem*. Make no mistake: this is not how the masters of Kabbalah *understand* the universe; rather, this is the way they *experience* it and then *describe* the experience.

If all existence is the endless light of *HaShem*, what are we?

For centuries science has been trying to figure out what we

are all made of. Scientists once thought that everything was composed of indestructible little balls called atoms. But, more recently, they discovered something quite revolutionary. They created a contraption that smashes elementary particles into each other to break them down in order to find the most basic building block of everything. Imagine if you wanted to know what a clock was made of. What would you do? You would take it apart or perhaps smash it into little pieces.

This is what scientists have been doing: they have been taking apart the world and smashing it to bits until they found the final bit that could not be broken down any further. Interestingly, when they smashed two elementary particles together they mysteriously got only more elementary particles. This is like smashing two clocks together with the expectation of finding screws and springs and instead getting more clocks.

This discovery led scientists to unite two principles of conservation that, until this point, they believed were separate and independent. There is a scientific principle called the conservation of mass. This principle states that there is no new mass in the universe and no old mass—mass is simply redistributed. There is a parallel principle called the conservation of energy, which states that there is no new or old energy, just the redistribution of energy.

These experiments show that mass is energy and energy is mass. When the particles smashed into each other, the energy in the momentum of the particles and the energy of the mass of the particles combined and redistributed to form more particles. As a result of these experiments, science now teaches that all is made of energy, and that energy is the basic building block of the entire universe.

But what really is energy? We talk about energy as if it is a thing, describing it as units. Science has proven, however, that energy is a dynamic process, a verb! Energy isn't a *what*, it is a *what's happening*. According to science, we are all a dynamic process, an event. We are not things, we are verbs.

The *Zohar* taught this concept long before science discovered it. The *Zohar* points out something very bizarre in the Torah. The Torah states, "Six days God created heaven and earth."[2] It doesn't say, "in" six days, rather it just says, "six days." So what's the difference?

The *Zohar* explains that the world was not created *in* six days but that the world *is* six days. The world and everything in it are made of time. But what is time? Time is also a process, an event. A day is a conceptual description of a segment of the process, like a movement in a musical score. A day is not a thing. It is a happening. The world wasn't created *in* six days—the world *is* six days. Therefore, the universe is a process, an event, a verb. We, as beings, are also verbs. But the noun or the subject is the Be-er, *HaShem*.

STAYING CONNECTED

When *HaShem* creates, He is not like a carpenter who builds a table, rather He is like a singer singing a song. When the carpenter finishes building the table he can leave the room and the table will continue to exist; the table's existence is not dependent upon its maker. But the song only continues as long

as the singer sings; and that is the nature of our relationship to
HaShem.

This idea actually explains one of the deeper meanings hidden in the Hebrew word *Israel*, as the Kabbalah illustrates. (One
of the favorite games of the Kabbalists is Scrabble; they take a
Hebrew word and scramble the letters to discover hidden mes-
sages expressed in the different combinations.) When Kabbalists rearrange the letters of the word *Israel*, they get the word
shirel, which means "the song of God." "The song of God" is hidden in the word *Israel* to illuminate the message that the Jewish
people are meant to bring to all of humanity—that we are all
part of a divine song. Each of us is a note in this incredible and
magnificent symphony played by the one and only musician.

When you understand this truth you will realize that nothing separates you from *HaShem*. If *HaShem* is like a singer, then
we are His song. If *HaShem* is like a dancer, then we are His
dance. Humanity and *HaShem* are never in conflict, nor are
they mutually exclusive opposites. The song is never separate
from its singer; the dance is never separate from its dancer. Remember, however, that the song *is not* the singer and the dance
is not the dancer. *They are one but not the same*.

According to Judaism, when you think you are a noun (instead of a verb), then you are denying yourself the awesome
feeling of being connected to your true source. From *HaShem's*
perspective, of course, you can never truly disconnect yourself
from the source, but from your perspective, it is what you
choose to do, and, therefore that is how you will experience
your life. You may not be able to put your finger on it, but you

will feel alienated and cut off. You will feel disconnected from the source of energy and life.

EXPERIENCING ONENESS

When you understand the true meaning of *HaShem* as the Be-er you will also look at the world differently. You will realize that everything and everyone is a manifestation of *HaShem*. Psalm 16 states: "I place YHVH before me always."[3] In other words, I always keep at the forefront of my mind that *HaShem* is the Be-er and the entire universe is His being. In fact, the path of Judaism empowers us to maintain consistently the awareness of this ecstatic truth.

When you become conscious of *being*, you see everyone within the universe as one—not one and the same, but as a perfectly harmonized symphony.

Imagine if a record producer were to say to Bach or Beethoven, "Your music is terrific. We would like to produce it, but we have some budgetary restrictions. Do you think you could cut out a couple of notes here and there?" What would the composer say? "A couple of notes! It will ruin the whole thing!" He would never agree to such a thing.

This is also *HaShem*'s attitude when we try to negate one of His notes. But that is essentially what we're doing when we speak slander about another person. If we speak against another person, we are saying that *HaShem* created someone who has no meaning, no importance, and no place in *HaShem*'s symphony. We are suggesting that in the divine symphony of life that person, that note, would not be missed.

The great eighteenth century teacher and founder of the Hassidic movement, the Baal Shem Tov, taught that our task in life is to realize that every one of us is a living manifestation of HaShem. We are all godly beings. There is never a separation between us, HaShem, or anyone else. The only question is whether we choose to experience that connection or whether we deny ourselves that pleasure, because staying connected is the true path to happiness.

True, there are people who seem to be happy without knowledge of, or interest in, HaShem. But I maintain that they could be a lot happier. They simply do not know that they could have a better life. It's as if they were color-blind; they're happy because they don't know anything about colors. But if they just got a glimpse of the splendor of colors, they would realize how much they were missing and how enriched their life could be.

Judaism offers a way to see deeper purples and brighter yellows in HaShem's masterpiece of life. Judaism empowers us to see and taste the colors and flavors of divine being, colors and flavors that we could have never dreamed existed without the guidance of the Torah.

JUDAISM AND SELF-ESTEEM

According to Judaism, we are truly happy when we are being who we are supposed to be. I'm really happy when I teach, because I know that I was meant to be a teacher. When I do something that does not fit the kind of being I am supposed to be, I don't feel happy. But when I feel connected to the source, and I am being the unique note that I'm supposed to be, I am happy.

It is unfortunate that many people do not trust who they are and are constantly comparing themselves to others, feeling jealous when they think somebody is better. If you ever find yourself feeling that way, remember that no one else is any more uniquely divine than you are. Perhaps someone is more beautiful or more intelligent than you are, but so what? Those are the notes that they are meant to be. They are no more or less a divine being than you are, and that is all that should matter.

A friend of mine who is a hairdresser once pointed out how people with curly hair want straight hair, people with straight hair want curly hair, people who are dark brown want to be blond, and blonds want to be redheads. It's amazing that all of these people pay a lot of money to be who they aren't. *HaShem* must have gotten it all wrong: the ones who are curly should have been straight, and the ones who are straight should have been curly.

We are simply not happy with who we are, because we don't really trust and believe that every one of us is a unique divine being, a holy note in the divine symphony. I'm a C-minor, you're a B, and she's a D-sharp. That's why we make such beautiful music together. If everyone were a C-minor, there would be no symphony, just monotony.

When you understand this, you cannot but honor and respect the vast differences among human beings, and you never want to be anyone other than who you are.

This is the goal of Judaism: to be who you are, a godly being.

4.

What Does God Want?

GOD WANTS US to be in sync with the flow of the universe.

For this reason God has given us a set of instructions—the mitzvot, the commandments of the Torah—as the most natural way of expressing who we are as godly beings. These instructions help us choreograph the dance serving the dancer, or compose the song serving the singer, who is God—*HaShem*.

Before we discuss how they do that, we must first explore what motivates human beings in general, that is, what drives us?

There are various psychological approaches to the source of motivation. Sigmund Freud, for example, said that our source of motivation is sex. Alfred Adler believed that the fundamental human drive is social acceptance, the need for honor.

Judaism disagrees. We learn from the *Ethics of the Fathers*, teachings from the oral tradition, that honor and sexual desire take a person "out of the world." In other words, they disorient us, damage our motivation, and undermine our success. From a Jewish point of view then, what drives human beings?

Simply put, we want to be who we are, godly beings. We seek to portray godliness through our thoughts, speech, and actions. We are driven to be like God because we are godly beings. For example, we seek to love because love portrays reality, the unity of God. We seek peace because peace portrays reality, the harmony of God. We aspire to put into action our values and ideals because they portray our inner godly essence. In other words, according to Judaism the source of human motivation is *emuna*. *Emuna*, as discussed in Chapter 2, means dedication to our essence and the successful portrayal of that truth in the world. We want to be godly beings, so we seek to express and portray godliness through our thoughts, speech, and actions.

The entire Torah lifestyle—which portrays who we are in our relationship to God and shows our dedication to God—is actually the fulfillment of *emuna*. Just as a successful artist is able to use paintbrushes to physically and truthfully express himself and portray what he believes, feels, and sees, so too, for a Jew, the mitzvot express his or her essence—godliness. The mitzvot are rooted in the power of *emuna*. They are the physical expressions of *emuna*.

THE REAL CHOICE

To want to be like God is not our *choice*, because we are created in the image of God—it's our natural inclination. Because of our *need* to be like God, we seek to transcend our limitations, just as the divine is transcendent of limitations. And just as God is omnipotent, we, too, want to experience this characteristic.

So, it is healthy and normal for us to strive for greatness. But we must ask ourselves whether we are portraying our godliness in an authentic way or in a counterfeit way. In Judaism, this is the real meaning of choice. We cannot help but want to be like God and experience our godliness. However, whether we truly achieve this is the result of the choices we make. We can do it in a genuine way or in a counterfeit way; we can choose to portray our true godliness by striving to emulate God's qualities, or we can choose to portray it falsely and act as if we are God.

We see counterfeit portrayals of godliness all the time, often when people try to exert control over others. Because God has power over everything, people, too, want to have power over everything.

Consider the man who dreams about being the chief executive officer of a huge company. As he moves up the corporate ladder and comes closer to the top, his dreams get bigger. Eventually he decides that being chief executive officer is not good enough, that instead he wants to take over all the shares and become owner of the company. What motivates him is the feeling of godliness in his actions. He thinks, "I am the boss. I am in control. I have it all."

Judaism teaches that even sinning is motivated by our need to portray godliness. The sin of the first man and woman is actually the archetype of all sin. When the snake came to them, he did not say, "You know what? If you eat of this tree you will be rich." Money, in essence, is really of no value to people. The snake also did not say, "If you eat of this tree, you will be famous, they will name apple juice after you." People really are not interested in fame. Nor did the snake say, "If you eat of this tree, you will have all your sexual desires fulfilled." Sex is not a true enticement to people. The only thing that motivated the first sin was to be like God. That is what the snake actually said. He told them, "If you eat of the tree you will be like God."[1]

This is really the only motivation that drives us all. We simply want to be who we are, god-like beings. But sometimes we confuse ourselves and think that material things will fulfill our godly aspirations. Money makes us feel independent, powerful, and self-sufficient—like a god. Fame tells us we are known, important, and significant—other god-like qualities. And sex can make us feel we are transcending our physical limitations; it expresses an urge to merge and feel part of a greater whole. While money, fame, and sex are all ways of trying to express and experience godliness, they are not authentic portrayals, and, if they are used in the wrong context, they may even become destructive.

Nobody is motivated to do wrong or commit evil. Wrongful actions are merely a by-product of trying to be god-like but in inauthentic ways. In our efforts to express godliness, we sometimes seek to control people and the events around us, and those efforts, in turn, become twisted. This is the problem of using counterfeit approaches to being god-like. And, of course, these counterfeit approaches can never satisfy our true desires.

I was watching the news one evening when the newscaster came on and said, "Ladies and gentleman, a truly unique and historic event is happening right now, and you can be part of it. We take you to our man, Joe, at the scene in Austria."

Joe appeared on the screen and said, "This is unbelievable.

This is great. I don't know why, but we have a bunch of people here who have just baked the longest apple strudel in the history of the world. Isn't this truly exciting?"

The newscaster said to him, "Wow! Could we get a close-up of the strudel, Joe?"

Watching this, I felt like I was landing on the moon. The camera was zooming across this apple strudel that did not seem to end.

Next thing, all the people put their faces up to the strudel. Then came the interviews, with people talking about their experiences with the strudel and why they wanted to be a part of this historic achievement.

Why do people do these things? The reason is because they have a desire to break world records and transcend limitations. But doing it with apple strudel? Why not go beyond your limitations and give a little more to charity or do more acts of kindness? Now that's godliness!

In the same way, this century's technological leaps may be a result of our desire to be like God and transcend the limitations of time and space. Years ago, we carried video cameras on our backs; this year we can hold them in the palms of our hands. It's progress, getting closer to what we are aspiring to achieve. Once upon a time, it took thirty hours to get across the world; now it takes fifteen hours. Next it will take seven hours, and then, "Beam me up, Scotty!"

What drives us to transcend time and space is our desire to be a manifestation of that which transcends time and space. But is this authentic? Is this significant? Is this the highest expression of our godliness, a direct portrayal of reality as it really is?

To portray our godliness authentically and in a truly meaningful way, we need to understand who we are in relationship to God.

SEPARATION, SERVICE, AND SONG

As explained in Chapter 3, there is no reality separate from God: God is reality, we exist within God, and God is manifest through us. So except in our minds and actions, we can never really separate ourselves from God. When we deny this truth by thinking and acting in discord with it, we experience pain— the pain of separation from God, who is our true source.

In the Book of Isaiah, the prophet tells the Jewish people, "Your wrongdoings have separated you from your God."[2] This is teaching us that if we experience separation from the source, it is only because of the mode of consciousness and lifestyle that we have chosen.

In reality, we are not independent beings; we are all living manifestations of God. Jewish consciousness promotes this fundamental concept through behavior, lifestyle, and speech —in essence, through obeying God's commandments and thus serving to manifest God in the world.

As mentioned earlier, according to the great Hassidic master the Baal Shem Tov, our goal in life is to realize that we are a manifestation of God. But "serving God" is a negative concept to many people, because they don't understand that God is the source of all being, all energy, and all creativity.

To understand this concept, imagine a time when you were completely engrossed in painting, singing, or another activity, to the point where you found yourself performing, quite naturally, on a much higher level. If you are a runner, remember those times when you felt like you couldn't go on, then all of a sudden something possessed you and drove you across the finish line. At times like these you'd wonder: Who did that? Did I do it? I was running but something else gave me the power to do it. Was I really the runner or the *running*?

Others might ask: Am I the *singing* or the singer? I think I am the painter, but am I really the *painting*? I know for myself that my best moments as a rabbi are when I know I am the just the *speaking*, not the speaker.

Serving God means being completely connected to our divine source and channelling divine presence into the world. That is what serving God means. Unfortunately, many people think "serving God" is submitting to an egomaniacal deity who dwells in heaven and demands, "You must serve me! Obey my commandments and do them with a smile! Or else I will punish you." In actuality, serving God is like the dance serving the dancer, the song serving the singer, the speech serving the speaker.

It is not a question of whether or not to serve. The question is *who* to serve. Serving another human being is enslavement, but serving the source of all life and creativity truly is liberation.

To serve God means striving to portray God's qualities of love, wisdom, understanding, kindness, justice, compassion, beauty, truth, peace, and so on. When we act mercifully, we are serving the source of all mercy. When we act intelligently, we are serving the source of all intelligence. And when we are serving justice, we are serving the source of all justice. This is how we authentically portray our godliness and experience true fulfillment. The path to ultimate meaning requires making our life a means to expressing God in the world.

Just how to make that path our own is explained in the Torah. In fact, Judaism makes an amazing claim—that living according to the mitzvot of the Torah is the most natural, authentic, and meaningful way to be who we really are.

The first man and woman were driven by their innate godliness to express and experience their true essence, but they didn't know the difference between the dance and the dancer. As humans, we are not the dancer; we are the dance. We may think that we're the dancer, but we can really only emulate the dancer and follow the steps God choreographs for us.

Asking why we would want to obey the commandments is like asking why the song would want to follow its singer or why the dance would want to follow its dancer. Judaism explains why: You are the creation, therefore, follow your Creator. And it is the mitzvot that enable us to do so in the most authentic, natural, and meaningful way—to express who we are as godly beings.

The Mitzvot

Because they do not understand that the mitzvot are our best portrayals of godliness, people think that Torah commandments are like Girl Scout cookies: if you sell them, at the end you get a prize. It is a very childish image of what the mitzvot represent.

The mitzvot are not simply ways to earn reward and avoid punishment. Rather, they are portrayals of our deepest *emuna*, derived from our ability to translate our relationship to God in the language of human behavior. If we were deeply connected to God, we would know the mitzvot intuitively.

According to Jewish tradition, it is for this reason that Abraham was able to fulfill all the mitzvot before God gave the Torah at Mt. Sinai. Abraham's awareness of, and connection to, God was so clear that his behavior portrayed that relationship and testified to his innate dedication to the source of his being. For Abraham, fulfilling the mitzvot was natural—just as was knowing the responsibilities implicit in the relationship between himself and his beloved.

If we were on Abraham's level, we too would know the responsibilities that portray our connection to God. But according to Judaism, without the Torah to guide us, we are not attuned to this truth. We need the responsibilities outlined in it to reconnect us.

And that is just what the mitzvot do. They keep us connected to God by spelling out the profound truth of our dedication to our source and the ultimate reality. All the details of the commandments are part of the painting of life, showing us how to portray our relationship and dedication to God. When we know this, it becomes easy to see how the mitzvot are reflecting our true selves in the deepest way.

EXPRESSING OUR TRUE ESSENCE

We are all looking for our own unique lifestyle that reflects and expresses ourselves in the world. And often we know that something is amiss.

Imagine that you feel that way and so you go to a handwriting analyst to help you find yourself. He looks at your handwriting and says, "This is very interesting. Could you bring me some of your art the next time we get together?"

"Art?" you ask. "I'm sorry, I'm not an artist, I'm an accountant."

"No, I can see in your handwriting that you are an artist," he tells you.

"No, no, no, I'm not an artist. Actually, I did want to be, but my parents insisted that I go to business school, and now I'm an accountant."

He then asks you to bring him some of your notebooks from college and when you do, he only smiles when he sees that you had drawn incredible doodles all over their pages. You had been trying to be an artist all through college, but somebody convinced you that you had to be an accountant.

"Therefore," the handwriting analyst says, "your mode of statement, the way you are going to be who you truly are, is by buying paint and a few paint brushes." He tells you that you need a studio and an easel, not an office and a computer, and that this is why you are feeling cut off. When you hold a pen or a brush, then you are connected. This is how Judaism describes the mitzvot: they connect us to our real selves and express our true identity.

The mitzvot guide us to do what we would naturally do if we knew our inner self. As such, they help put us in touch with our true essence as divine beings. For this reason, the Torah refers to Moses as *Moshe Rabbeinu* ("Moses our Teacher") and Jacob as *Yaakov Aveinu* ("Jacobo our Father"). These titles express the essence of these great people and what they have contributed to the evolution of the Jewish people. A father passes on many of his traits, while a teacher gives us ways to express who we are. The *Zohar* says that the Torah that Moses brought us from God is a way of life that empowers us to express who we are genetically, as children of Jacob.

When people ask me why they should be Jewish, my question is, "Are you Jewish?" Because if you are genetically Jewish—why not be Jewish? I don't understand the question "Why be Jewish?" It is like asking me, "Why be a redhead?" I *am* a redhead, so why not *be* a redhead?

Therefore, the real question is, "Am I Jewish?" If that is the kind of being that I am, if that is the note that I am in the symphony of God, then why not be that note? If I'm a D-sharp, why try to be a C? It makes no sense.

The great Master of Kabbalah, Rabbi Isaac Luria, who was known as the Ari, had an amazing way of diagnosing people. He would have them visualize the Hebrew letters making up YHVH. As people closed their eyes and visualized the letters, they described them very differently. Some described seeing turquoise letters or purple letters or white letters on black fire. Some people had a problem seeing some of the letters or parts of the letters, while others could see them all at the same time.

Some said the letters popped in and out. Based on his subjects' visualization, the Ari would diagnose exactly what was wrong and which mitzvah they had neglected.

The Ari's exercise shows that we are meant to be living expressions of YHVH. We are meant to live our lives in ways that reveal the truth of God to the world. By visualizing God's name, we can see whether we are a living portrayal of the divine. Our success in being a statement of the divine is indicated by our ability to visualize it. Our ability to portray it in our mind's eye is a reflection of how well we portray it in our daily life. As divine beings, portraying the divine is our job in this world and our way to personal fulfillment.

The Ari's mystical process of diagnosis showed that the extent to which his subjects could visualize the letters was also the extent to which they were able to portray God in their lives. Based on their visualization, the Ari could understand their level of *emuna*—their dedication to God—and their successful portrayal of that dedication.

This teaches us that what we are actually doing when we are praying, studying Torah, or fulfilling the other mitzvot is spelling out God's name in the world, so to speak. The more we can project God in the world, the more we will be able to visualize God's name in our mind's eye and the better able we will be to live according to our true essence. When we do not fulfill the mitzvot—or worse, when we violate the mitzvot—we betray our soul and inner truth.

AVOIDING SELF-BETRAYAL

Being disloyal to your inner truth is how Judaism defines transgression. When I walk down the street and see somebody abuse another human being I know that something is wrong, because the person's act is completely incongruent with his inner godly self and how he should be expressing himself in the world. According to Judaism, these betrayals are transgressions. They are born of a lifestyle that is not dedicated to God or the successful portrayal of that relationship and who we are.

According to the Kabbalah, when we fulfill a mitzvah, we are uniting the letters of God's name, and when we commit a transgression, we are severing the letters. This does not mean that we remove God's name from the world—we just make it unreadable. God is in the world no matter what we do. But when we behave in discord with the mitzvot, we make God's presence unreadable and incomprehensible. Conversely, when we behave in a way that portrays *emuna*, we become a vehicle for expressing God and strengthening His manifestation in the world.

Remember, we are not self-defined. Knowing who we are is a function of the unique relationship that we have with God. Therefore, when we betray our relationship with God, we are ultimately betraying ourselves. It is for this reason that when Adam sinned, he and Eve ran and hid behind a bush. As the Torah relates, God called out to Adam and said, "Where are you?" The question was rhetorical. What God was really saying to Adam and Eve was, "Where are *you*? You betrayed yourself."

Our transgressions are self-betrayals. They not only fail to manifest God in the world, they also prevent us from expressing who we really are. Our transgressions betray us, because they betray who we are in relationship to God. All wrongdoing is based on being someone we're not.

The Midrash relates a parable about the sin of the moon, who wanted to be something it was not. The moon wanted to be like the sun, which was bigger and more prominent. The moon was not ready to accept its unique relationship to the source; as a result it betrayed itself and was punished.

Self-betrayal is an ongoing problem of the Jewish people, reoccurring in various biblical stories and in Jewish history in general. The mistake many Jews make is that they want to be accepted by the rest of the world and they think this can be accomplished by imitating the other peoples. Unfortunately many Jews today are not proud to be Jewish. What they do not realize, however, is that every nation has a different role in the world and a unique way of serving God and manifesting godliness. Only when we all come to respect our differences and proudly embrace our unique mission will peace fill the earth.

When Jews understand that being Jewish is who they really are, they will be better able to express themselves, serve God, and improve the world. Only when they connect themselves to the spiritual destiny of the nation of Israel will they be able to see clearly the great truth that is contained in the Torah, in Jewish traditions, and even in Jewish customs.

CULTURE AND CUSTOM

Like the mitzvot, Jewish customs are also part of Torah. According to Judaism, there is an idea that if the Jewish people do something in a customary way, then it becomes obligatory like the commandments. It's an amazing idea that custom can take on the obligation of Jewish law. For example, the Torah does not specifically state that we should wear a *kippa* or *yarmulke* (skull cap), but wearing one has become a cultural manifestation of Jewish identity and thus has become as obligatory as Torah law.

There are various other customs that Jewish people keep according to their cultural heritage, such as those accepted by Sephardim (the Jews who lived in the Middle East) and Ashkenazim (the Jews who lived in Europe). Both groups follow customs that you would not find in Jewish law but that hold great importance. Judaism teaches that if a custom has become a way to manifest Jewishness, then, like a mitzvah, it helps us portray our true self.

Because the mitzvot portray the essence of the Jewish people and their unique relationship with God, Jews do not encourage non-Jews to fulfill mitzvot. Non-Jews have a different kind of relationship with God, expressed in and portrayed through different kinds of responsibilities as spelled out by the Torah. These are grouped under the Seven Mitzvot of the Children of Noah and consist of the commandments that God gave to the entire world after the Flood. Of course, there are non-Jews who feel a unique connection to the Jewish community, and that connection may indicate that Judaism is their true way of portraying their essence and godliness in the world; these non-Jews may eventually convert. But as creations of God, Jews and non-Jews both express godliness, even if each group plays a different role in the world and each expresses its relationship to God differently.

According to the Torah, the Seven Mitzvot of the Children of Noah are the tools of the non-Jews for expressing their godliness authentically. Today there are more and more non-Jews who are becoming interested in exploring these seven mitzvot and are finding fulfillment in doing so.

EMBRACING THE TRUE SELF

Whether a Jew or a non-Jew, anyone with a moral sensitivity is likely to embrace the mitzvot eventually, once that person understands that these commandments from God actually support and facilitate what his or her inner self truly wants to accomplish.

I recently got a call from a woman I had not spoken to in many years. She said that she had been in psychiatric care and was thinking of killing herself. As I was trying to figure out why she suddenly thought to call me, she said, "You know, I have no religion in my life." I then realized that this was why she was calling me. I was a rabbi.

Without any religious context for her life, I could understand why she was feeling totally lost. When I told her this, she said, "But I'm not a religious person, and I don't keep Shabbat. I don't even light Shabbat candles."

I said to her, "You don't have to keep Shabbat in order to light Shabbat candles. You can just start lighting Shabbat candles."

I was not saying that she should not keep Shabbat; I was just telling her that she should not feel that Judaism is all or nothing. If she started with just lighting Shabbat candles, that would be a way of connecting with God and starting the journey toward a more meaningful life and greater personal fulfillment.

That is what happens: many people become lost because they have no idealistic framework to their lives. They cut God out of their lives. People who ask themselves if it really matters whether or not they believe in God have no understanding of God. They think that God has nothing to do with them, and that life can go on happily without God. The very foundation and context of our life is God, and our inner drives are only going to be satisfied in the context of serving God.

A life of mitzvot will give these people exactly what they are looking for. It will support their inner drive and give them vitality and joy. But most people think the opposite, and they run from mitzvot because they are afraid of commitment. If they understood that the mitzvot bring one back to one's self, they would embrace the commitment joyfully.

When we separate ourselves from God, and when we deny God, we ultimately deny our true self, the self that seeks a life built on ideals. A return to our true inner self is ultimately a return to God. Eventually people come to understand this, but most first have to feel lost.

If you are a moral being, a person who cares about doing what is right, then you are a person who finds fulfillment in knowing that you are a means to a higher end. You will find, if you have not already, that Torah and the mitzvot will give you the necessary guidance.

An unfortunate problem today is that many people have no idea about this, and further they have no idea what it means to fulfill mitzvot.

When we live according to Torah, we're connecting with a higher perspective on life. We're seeing the bigger picture and behaving in a manner that expresses and reflects what reality truly is, even if we do not completely perceive it. When we live the mitzvot, we behave in a way that is harmonious with the way life truly is. And we are rewarded with living according to our true essence. Then we enjoy a meaningful life and experience ultimate personal fulfillment.

5.

What Is Torah?

IF YOU ASK PEOPLE to define the Torah, you will hear a lot of strange ideas. I've heard people say that it's the Jewish book of rituals and ethics, and that it's an archaic tome full of legends. Many people say that because the Torah was written thousands of years ago, it is irrelevant today. Others say it is restrictive and suppressive, and who wants to give up the fun things in life to live as a "slave" to God?

The people who say this have it all wrong. The Torah is not simply a book of interesting philosophical or mystical concepts. Torah is a set of beliefs regarding the nature of reality—man, life, and the beyond.

Judaism claims that these beliefs express what God believes and how God acts. And when we model ourselves after God—as the Torah teaches us to do—we, too, become godly. We, too, become holy, just as God is holy: "Holy you shall be, because I, the Lord Your God, am holy."[1]

BOOK OF LIFE

King Solomon in his book of Proverbs describes the Torah poetically as a Tree of Life:

She is a tree of life to those who grasp her; and happy is everyone who holds her fast. Her ways are ways of pleasantness, and all her paths are peace.[2]

Most of us know that in the Garden of Eden there stood two trees: the tree of knowledge, from which Adam and Eve were not allowed to eat and the tree of life, which stood in the middle of the garden.[3] When they ate from the tree of knowledge, they chose death and brought mortality into the world.

But though they were banished from the garden, we as their descendants got a second chance to eat from the tree of life when we received the Torah at Mt. Sinai. As Moses told the Jews while they were wandering in the desert: "I have placed before you life and death, blessing and curse. Choose life. . . ."[4]

In short, the Torah is a path to life.

But if the Torah is about life, then what is life? If we don't know, we have no way of knowing what it is that the Torah, with its instructions for living, is trying to teach us to do.

Imagine that you are walking down the street and you find an instruction book, but the first page is ripped out. You really won't know what the book is about. The first chapter is called "Diet for Success." Success in what, you do not know. The chapter starts with a long list of what you can't eat: no soda, French fries, burgers, and so forth. It goes on and on about what you can't eat and then ends by telling you to eat three yogurts a day with some orange juice. You think, "This is horrible! Why would I do this?"

So you go to the next chapter, "Exercises for Success." Success in what? You do not know. It describes excruciating exercises in which you put your leg up on a bar a hundred times a day. (Nothing about explaining this to the bartender though.) You quickly turn to the next chapter, hoping that it's more interesting and fun. It's entitled "Proper Dress." There you see a person dressed in what looks like a skin suit. It is embarrassing. You would never walk down the street in that. This is ridiculous.

Just as you are about to throw the manual in the trash, someone comes up to you and says, "Oh, I see that you found the book."

"Yes, and I was about to trash it," you say.

"But it's a great book!" he exclaims.

"It is?"

And he begins cleverly to prove that every word of it is true.

Now imagine that you followed that manual without knowing that it is really about success in dancing. Without knowing the simplest and most important word, "*dance*," would you ever learn how to dance from the manual?

Similarly if you don't know what life is, you are likely puzzled by the Torah and what it is guiding you to do.

LIFE AS DEFINED BY GOD

When Isaac Newton proposed his law of universal gravitation in the seventeenth century, he had not *invented* gravity, he had merely *discovered* it. Gravity is a force that has been dictating the movement of physical bodies since the beginning of time. Once he understood this, Isaac Newton was able to articulate a principle, thus describing a force through which God directs the world.

Albert Einstein formulated his unified field theory because he believed there must be a consistent set of such principles governing the movement of life. As he put it, "God does not play dice with the universe."

We naturally live in accordance with the laws of physics, such as gravity. It is obvious to all that it would be absurd for us to oppose them. But whether or not we accept gravity does not make a difference to its existence or to its influence upon us; gravity does not ask our opinion. It was, is, and will be. To deny it and try to live against this or any other physical principle is akin to committing suicide.

But if there are physical principles that govern our existence, perhaps there are also spiritual/moral principles. And just maybe, as definitive as the law of gravity, the laws of conservation of mass and energy, and others, there are laws like "Thou shall not swap wives even if you are consenting adults."

Are morals and ethics a matter of consensus or social contract, or are they established laws of the universe? Before you answer, think of it this way: If Adolf Hilter had convinced the entire world that it is right to murder Jews, and in a democratic referendum the whole world voted that it is right to murder Jews, would that have made it good and right? Or would it have been wrong no matter what? Does the majority rule in all matters?

Judaism teaches that the spiritual and moral dimension of

life is no different from the physical dimension. And, like gravity and other laws of nature, there are spiritual and ethical laws,
which govern the nature of our spiritual life. These laws have
been guiding the universe since its very inception.

Judaism teaches that God created the world in accordance
with the principles and laws spelled out in the Torah. It also
states that Adam and Eve were originally naturally in sync
with the flow of life. They intuited the laws of the Torah, but
the snake confused them and they lost their natural connection. During the time of Noah, there was a possibility for a mass
revelation of the Torah's eternal laws, but that generation was
not ready or willing. Abraham was so attuned to his soul and
the inner core of all being, that he intuitively followed the details of Torah law. In fact, we all know the Torah—it is encoded
in our souls—but we forget it as soon as we are born, when we
become preoccupied with the needs and wants of our bodies.
Therefore, 3,300 years ago, when the entire Jewish people
stood at Mt. Sinai waiting for a revelation of the Torah, they
already knew it subconsciously.

At Sinai that subconscious knowledge became conscious.
The universal principles of spirituality, morality, and ethics
were revealed to them, along with specific instructions regarding the particular Jewish role and responsibility in the scheme
of creation. The Torah they received contained the divine
principles and laws that had always directed life. But it was
only then that the Jewish people were ready and willing to accept them.

WHAT YOU KNOW

There are many Torah principles to which you already are naturally attuned. For example, most people don't need to be told, "Thou shall not have bestial relations."

But imagine that times have changed and people have lost this natural sense of right and wrong. Let's say you are sitting in your living room watching television when your daughter comes in excited.

"Mom, Dad!" she beams. "I'm engaged!"

"Who's the fellow?" you ask. "Is he Jewish? What's he like?"

"He's just fantastic!"

She opens the door and in walks a horse. You are beside yourself. "He's a horse!" you yell. "Are you nuts!?!"

Your daughter stares at you. "I thought you were open minded! You've always taught me to find my own way. Now you've probably hurt his feelings. And he's the nicest guy I've ever met!"

What would you say at this point? Would you say it is wrong to have relations with a horse? Would you say that there is a certain way that things are done and a certain way that life is lived, and this is not one of them? But if she has lost this innate sense, she will probably look at you and not understand.

Let's say you decide to send your daughter to a psychiatrist, whom you pay $300 an hour to discuss the problem with her. She tells him that there is nothing wrong with her, and it is her parents who really need his help. They are the ones obsessing over the fact that she is engaged to a horse. The psychiatrist says to her, "Happiness means accepting who you are, and if this is who you are, then everyone should accept your decision. It's a free world and you are not hurting anyone." Your daughter comes home and says, "Mom, Dad! I'm really happy, because the psychiatrist told me that he is also engaged to a horse and that it's okay."

At this point, you would say to yourself, "Why is it so clear to me that nobody should ever marry a horse? It's just not the way things are!" But your daughter is wondering what is wrong with you. It is difficult to articulate that this is a given principle, like gravity, that we simply cannot go against. And if we do we will only bring ruin upon ourselves. But that is the only true response.

Not everyone believes that the Torah embodies the truth. But remember we are talking about basic principles that have existed from the beginning of time. Whether you articulate them correctly or incorrectly does not affect the existence of the principles. Therefore, we must all seek the truth, so that we can all align our lives with the principles and live in harmony with the design of the universe.

UNIVERSAL PRINCIPLES

Through stories and precepts, the Torah articulates the exact divine principles that govern life and gives us the mitzvot, which are particular actions that are tailored to accord with those principles.

To choose to follow the Torah and abide by these principles—both the ones we know innately and the ones we may not yet understand—is to choose a life of freedom, as the Torah explicitly states.

The Torah, in the Book of Exodus, tells us, "And the tablets were the work of God, and the writing was the writing of God, engraved upon the tablets."⁵ The Hebrew word that can be translated as "engraved," *charut,* also means "freedom." There-fore, the sages explain that the words engraved on the tablets are our true source of personal freedom.

Many people, however, look at the Torah and mistakenly think, "It won't let me be open minded and free." This is a common misconception. What these people do not realize is that living in tandem with the very forces that guide the world frees us from having to struggle against them. It prevents stress and dis-ease.

AN AGENT
FOR SELF-EMPOWERMENT

When God offered the Torah to the Jews, they recognized that God was presenting the principles upon which life has been functioning since its very inception. Their first response was, "We will do it."⁶ They did not try to figure out whether the Torah fit their values, nor did they expect God to conform to their standards. Rather they wanted to conform to God's stan-dards. In so doing, they experienced the great pleasure, the reward, of living in harmony with divine values and ideals. They understood that the Torah was, is, and always will be the guiding force of the universe at the core of all being. They re-alized that the principles and the mitzvot of the Torah would empower them to be who they were supposed to be: godly beings living in harmony with life and at one with God.

In the Garden of Eden the snake convinced Adam and Eve that conforming to God's will and obeying His command was self-diminishing. The snake's message was: "Do your own thing, be your own god. You can set your own standards for what is good and bad. You do not have to subordinate yourself by accepting the rules of God."

But the Jewish people understood that the Torah is not self-diminishing, it is self-fulfilling; this is why they accepted the Torah without question. After all, is it self-diminishing to align yourself with the force of gravity? On the contrary, it is empowering to know and adhere to the laws of gravity. By knowing this universal principle, you can design a rocket and travel into outer space to, perhaps, discover new worlds. Similarly, knowing the ethical and spiritual laws of the universe enables you to connect with the guiding force of life and in so doing achieve freedom.

There are two kinds of freedom: freedom from oppression and freedom of expression. When the Jews left Egypt, they were freed from oppression and subordination by a human ruler, the Pharaoh. However, when they received the Torah at Mt. Sinai, they reached a new level of freedom, the freedom to be who they were. They became free to express their essence, to actualize their potential, and to live in joyous harmony with the universe and with God.

When the Jewish people accepted the Torah, they did not feel a conflict between their will and God's will. They realized that God is the source of all being and all will. He is the singer and we are His song. He is the dancer and we are His dance. Realizing this at Mt. Sinai, the Jews said, "We will do and then we will understand."[7] In other words, through doing, we will experientially understand how personally fulfilling it really is to align our will with God's will.

The Midrash teaches that God offered the Torah to all the nations existing at that time but they refused it. These nations did not understand the true meaning of Torah. They felt imposed upon, thinking that living according to the principles and laws of the Torah would lead to self-denial. They did not realize that it would be just the opposite—as the Jews have since demonstrated and as Judaism teaches to this day.

Sadly, I have found that many Jews feel like the nations who rejected the Torah: they feel that a Jewish lifestyle is contrary to who they are. They can't imagine how living life according to the dictates of Torah could be a key to personal freedom. To them it is far from a tree of life but rather a life sentence in a prison. These Jews either don't know the Torah or misinterpret it, reading into it something it is not.

RETURNING TO TORAH

When I first tasted authentic Judaism, when I finally experienced what it was really all about, I found that it deeply resonated within me. When I decided to live according to the Torah, I felt more myself than I ever had.

In Judaism, there is no need to be born again. Once was good enough! There is no idea of suddenly becoming a different person. All you have to do is go back to who you originally were. That is why the Jewish word for repentance is *teshuva* (literally "return"). The *baalei teshuva*—people who return to authentic Judaism—share an interesting feeling, a feeling that they are so much more in touch with their original essence. They realize that in their previous lifestyle, they were alienating themselves from their inner essence, and that now they have returned to themselves.

What bothered some of my friends when I began to incorporate Jewish practices into my life was their hope that I would become weird. They expected me to lose my sense of humor, to talk funny and to walk funny. They were challenged when they saw that I was the same person and yet not the same person. But not only could they still relate to me as I was doing these strange Jewish things, I seemed to be even more grounded and in touch with myself than ever. And that is exactly how I felt. Although I gave up cheeseburgers and Friday night at the movies, I have never felt that I was denying myself any of the true joys in life. It has actually been quite the opposite: I have only gained. I have lost nothing, and I found myself.

So I can personally assure you: the Torah is not a book of old stories or annoying precepts; it articulates the universal principles of spiritual and ethical life and empowers you to be who you really are. It frees you to live in harmony with the universe and at one with God.

6.
Why Study Torah?

WHY STUDY TORAH? Because to live a meaningful life attuned to our soul's essence, we must.

But before we explore how Torah study helps us do that, we need to understand the true purpose of learning and education. What I am about to share applies not only to Jewish education but to education in general, whether religious or secular in nature, because when education veers away from its true purpose it becomes (at best) a vehicle for cramming information into the head of the student, or, (far worse) nothing more than indoctrination.

As a child I was exposed to both. Growing up in Toronto, I attended a secular elementary school and high school, as well as Hebrew evening school at the local Conservative synagogue.

I was a hard-working student who diligently tried to finish essays and studied like mad for exams. I have poor long-term memory and difficulty retaining facts. But my short-term memory is good, so I would cram at the last minute, frantically trying to absorb all the information I was trying to learn.

Sometimes after a night of cramming, just before dozing off to sleep, haunting questions would surface from inside me:

What am I doing here? Why am I studying? Who do I want to be in life? Why do I exist?

Most of us have these same questions, though they arise at different points in our lives. And we often neglect giving them the time required for finding the answers.

For me, the questions arose during high school, where I got high marks only because of my ability to memorize a mass of information. I often heard, "Oh, boy, this guy has a future. He could be a doctor. He could be a lawyer. He could be an accountant." On the outside, I was considered a success, but on the inside I was a confused adolescent. My high marks hid the fact that twenty percent of the information I crammed into my head popped out as soon as I finished a test. Three or four hours later, another ten percent vanished, and in a day or two another ten percent disappeared. Looking back now, I hardly remember any of it.

Besides being evaluated on knowledge retention, I was also graded on my ability to solve analytical problems in math and physics. But my high marks hardly indicated what kind of person I was. Could I become a great doctor if I was not a caring person? Could I become a brilliant lawyer if I was not just and fair? Could I even become a decent human being if I had never been taught to deal with life's big issues, ideals, values, and ethics?

I wondered how my so-called education was going to help solve my inner questions and make me a good person. There was little or nothing in my education that promoted personal growth or self-discovery. Little I learned in school prepared me to be a sensitive, loving husband or father. As I was busy memorizing vast quantities of knowledge, I knew the least about the *knower* of the knowledge—me.

The only class in high school that related to my adolescent angst was sex education, a subject uppermost in my mind at the time. This class was taught by the gym teacher, whom I'll call Mr. McCallen. Mr. McCallen was not an impressive intellectual. In fact, he made it clear that he became a gym teacher by default, after realizing he would never be a hockey star. For one year, my class listened to Mr. McCallen's lectures about intimate relations between men and women. My friend Sheldon, who sat next to me in every class, told me repeatedly that Mr. McCallen's information was all mixed up; and it turned out that Sheldon was right.

Aside from Mr. McCallen and his dubious lectures, there was no one in my high school who addressed anything that was important to me on a personal or soul level: questions such as "Who am I?" and "Why am I?"

Shouldn't the main concern of education be to address these types of questions?

Forbidden Subjects

It was not until much later in life that I realized why a public high school had to be this way. My key insight came from working for a Jewish youth organization that hired me after concluding that it was failing to impart a Jewish identity to its members. They decided to try an experiment and hire someone with actual knowledge of Judaism to conduct programs dealing with Jewish issues.

For one of my programs I invited a group of teenagers for a fun weekend celebrating Shabbat. On Shabbat afternoon, I announced to them the hour-long break, "Okay, you can do whatever you want to do." I did not realize how loaded that statement was. "Whatever you want" was translated into sex. When I found out, I split them up and gave them a serious talk about appropriate behavior.

The next day at the office I was confronted by my boss, who was already somewhat threatened by me, because she was directing a Jewish organization while not believing in Judaism herself. "I heard you had a problem in your program," she said to me.

"Problem? No problem," I said. "You know, boys will be boys and girls will be girls."

"And so? What did you do?"

"I dealt with it."

"And *that's* the problem," she accused. "You dealt with it absolutely wrong."

"What did I do wrong?" I humbly asked.

"You moralized to them. You can't do that kind of thing around here."

This was a very strange thing to say to a rabbi. For what were they paying me? Why did they hire a rabbi?

So I asked, "Could you tell me what exactly I should have said?"

She said, "You should have told them that their behavior was against the constitution of the organization and forbidden on any of our seminars. But you should not have told them that their behavior was morally inappropriate. That's for their *parents* to tell them, not you."

I was really amazed. I felt like resigning because as a rabbi my job is to make moral statements and inspire people to grow ethically and spiritually. But suddenly, at that moment, I remembered an incident that happened to me when I was a child that helped me understand the confines of the system and the obstacles to education.

When I was in second grade, the school day started with everyone reciting the Lord's Prayer. After that we would sing "God Save the Queen." Why Canadians still wanted their kids to sing about saving the queen is beyond me. But one day we walked into class and our teacher said, "Class, legislation has just been passed in the government."

We looked at each other, wondering what is "legislation," a kind of ice cream? In grade two, what do you know?

"There was legislation passed in government that does not allow anything of a religious nature into the school system," our teacher explained. "Therefore, we will no longer say the Lord's Prayer." After so many years, there would be no more prayers in the school system. "And now class," the teacher continued, "please stand and sing 'God Save the Queen.'"

(Funny. We were not allowed to talk about God or pray to God, but whoever this God is, could He please, finally, save the queen.)

Remembering this incident clarified for me why there was a conscientious effort to remove from the educational system anything religious—and along with it anything moral/spiritual

—which might help the student answer the great existential questions every human being confronts from time to time.

Parents do not believe that religion belongs in school, because they see it as a personal matter. For this reason, I believe, public school courses avoid covering *any* life issue—because any life issue is a religious issue. Whether it is this kind of mineral or that kind of rock, no parent can come and argue, "Geology is against my religion." But talk about "Rock of Ages" —now that's something completely different! So the school system removed anything that would create religious tension. (The funny thing is that schools continue to cover evolution, as if the theory does not have religious repercussions.)

Thus schools have become very good at cramming their students' heads full of facts, but are forced to abdicate the responsibility of addressing the core ethical and spiritual issues that are essential for their students' becoming better human beings and living more meaningful lives.

Judaism, however, sees education as having a completely different role. The Hebrew word for education, *chinuch*, gives us a clue. *Chinuch* is associated with the Hebrew word *chen*, which means "grace." When you meet people with *chen*, you realize there is something very attractive about them. But *chen* is not the same as "pretty," which is *yofi* in Hebrew.

We all have had the experience of meeting someone whose face seemed beautiful only to have this first impression quickly wear off as we heard that person complain, criticize, and spew out negativity. Similarly, we all have had the experience of meeting someone who did not seem at all attractive at first glance but who became beautiful when he or she broke into a smile or demonstrated kindness and warmth.

That sort of experience demonstrates the difference between *chen* and *yofi*. *Yofi* is an external beauty. *Chen* is inner beauty. You may be wondering what all of this has to do with *chinuch*, education. *Chinuch* means to draw out a person's inner beauty, a beauty that is a function of relationship. It translates into how well you relate to yourself, your friends, your community, the world, and the reality beyond all, which we call God. Through the relationship and its harmony, an inner beauty will emerge.

This kind of education is what Torah study is all about. The Talmud (Eruvin 54b) praises the Torah for bringing *chen* upon all who study it.

EDUCATION VS. INDOCTRINATION

The word *education* comes from the Latin word *educare*, which means to "draw out." To educate, therefore, means to draw out something that fundamentally is already there. In the process of education, you actually become aware of yourself. You grow, you transform and become the real you. Rather than simply memorizing a bunch of information, you absorb ideas that draw out the inner you and bring you into the world of harmonious relationships. As you discover your own inner beauty of *chen*, you discover the *chen* of all people from the interrelatedness we all share.

Indoctrination is the complete opposite of education, though a lot of indoctrination masquerades as education. Indoctrination seeks to put something into you, while education tries to bring something out of you.

At the very early stages of education, we send our children to kindergarten, *gan* as it is called in Hebrew. Kindergarten comes from the German and literally means "children's garden" (*gan* also means "garden"). What kind of name is this for a children's school? A better name would be "kinder-workshop" or "kinder-factory." But if education is likened to a garden, then the educator is really a spiritual gardener. A gardener interacts with a seed. If he has a pear seed, then he wants to identify it as a pear seed so he can nurture it into a pear tree. If she has a carrot seed, she will want to nurture it into a carrot.

In other words, an educator's job is to create an environment that feeds you ideas that will nourish you in a manner in which you will grow and flourish. A good educator only wants you to be who you are.

While an educator is like a gardener, an indoctrinator is like a carpenter. A carpenter imposes his vision on a raw material, while a gardener sets his vision according to his seed; whatever you are, he wants you to become.

To indoctrinate is to coerce. It involves imposing the teacher's values—aspirations, identity, and character—on the student, so that the student will become like the teacher and reflect the teacher. In the process of indoctrination, a conflict is liable to arise between the teacher and the student, because the teacher has a message he or she wants the student to accept, even at the expense of the student's unique identity and individuality. Because the teacher may be physically or men-

tally more powerful than the student, he or she is able to coerce the student to bend and submit to the teacher's position.
There are teachers who are brilliant in their logic yet coercive
in their brilliance, rather than concerned about the student's
growth. Conversely, the educational process starts first with a
genuine caring relationship with the student.

To educate also is to communicate. Communication is not
simply two people taking turns speaking. It can be one person
listening and the other person speaking. What's the difference?
The word *communication* is from the same source as the word
community. In an indoctrination experience, the teacher is imposing himself or herself on the student. The object is to impose the teacher's views in such a way that they become the
student's own view. However, in an educational experience,
the object is to communicate truth. Therefore, the teacher's
message will resonate from without and from within the student. The message the student hears is something that he or
she would have heard from inside had he or she been open to
it or had someone helped him or her to be open to it.

When you hear truth it resonates inside, not just outside.
And there is something inside that tells you that you knew it
all along. To indoctrinate is to *impose*, but to educate is to *expose* what is inside. The educator is simply sharing truth.

This is especially true when is comes to Torah education.
The Talmud teaches that when we are in our mother's womb,
we are taught the entire Torah. But just as we are about to be
born an angel touches us over our upper lip and we forget it all.
In other words, Torah education is not a process of discovery

but *recovery*. True Torah education empowers us to reclaim the inner truth we already know.

TORAH: EDUCATION PAR EXCELLENCE

Torah study is a profound way to draw out the knowledge in the depths of our soul to understand the truth we already know. The purpose of Torah study is not, therefore, to memorize a bunch of facts and cram them into our heads. It is to expose the inner truth and our spiritual *chen*, the inner beauty that permeates reality through our relationship with it. For this reason, the Torah is called a book of life and *not* a book of knowledge.

A book of life is very different from a book of knowledge. Let's say that the best expression of your essence is for you to be a doctor, but someone gives you a book about oil painting. To you, that book would be a book of knowledge. It would give you information about painting, but it would not nurture you, reflect the real you, draw out your essence, or give you guidance to relate to the world. If you would give that same book to an artist, however, it would be a book of life. It would feed him, draw him out, and direct him to effectively be himself and relate to the world in his special individual way.

As we saw in the previous chapter, the Torah is a book of life because what is written in the Torah is not simply knowledge. It is much more than that. In fact, Judaism claims that the text of the Torah is crucial to our growth. The Torah gives us guidance to relate to ourselves, others, the world and, of course, the ultimate reality we call God.

Thus Torah study is a process of self-actualization. It is a process of becoming true to ourselves, as a seed becomes a blossoming tree. This is the essence and goal of a true educational process. Jewish education is based on the assumption that you are, in your essence, a Jew and the truths of Torah are already encoded in your soul. Judaism teaches that a Jew is not simply a product of sociological or cultural evolution, a person who simply likes bagels and chicken soup and lives in a certain kind of place. Rather, Judaism teaches that a Jew is a particular kind of soul, and that each individual soul is born with a certain disposition and role that it plays in the world.

Judaism says that if you were born a Jew, then you are a Jew. Whether you like it or not, know it or not, and whether you even care, that is who you are. To actualize that part of yourself you need to be educated to its meaning. And therefore Jewish education is concerned with helping you closely explore your life in a way that will help you live according to your unique Jewish essence and the Torah truths encoded in your soul. Doing so will help you reclaim your true self. And the more you are you, the more profoundly beautiful will be all the relationships you engage in—whether with your fellow human beings or with God.

A Living and Loving Encounter

Now before you dive headfirst into Torah study, a word of caution. You can't just read Torah or study it in the same way you read and study other books or subjects. It is important that you align your expectations with what is really being offered so that you don't set yourself up for failure and disappointment.

Imagine a fellow who's really excited about attending a rock concert who mistakenly finds himself in a theater where a symphony orchestra is playing. His reaction is disappointment. Everybody else in the theater is happy, because they are getting what they came for. But he came expecting something completely different.

To appreciate what you're getting, you have to know what you're being offered. This is true not only about Torah study but about Judaism in general.

I once heard a little fable about the dove that illustrates this point. In its early evolutionary stages, the dove didn't have wings; it only walked. And it was a delicacy to a lion.

One particular dove had great trouble evading an especially tenacious pursuer. The lion would run after the dove, and the dove would barely get away. So the dove prayed to God: "Please God, can't you help me? I'm a poor little dove and I can hardly outrun this lion."

The next day, the dove found that her prayers had been answered: she had been given wings. Now she was feeling very confident. The next day when she saw the lion, she began to tease him, "Hey pussycat, over here. I'm not afraid of you, I've got wings."

She allowed the lion to get close to her because she wanted to show off. When the lion was within reach, she laughed and started running down the street. But the wings were heavy, and they slowed her down. The dove tried to run faster and faster, but it proved impossible for her to get away. She tripped over her wings and, well, you can guess what happened next. I will save you the gory details.

When the dove got up to heaven, she complained to God, "I don't understand, I prayed to You, I asked for Your help and this is what You did to me? You gave me these clumsy wings?" God answered, "Dove, I didn't give you those wings to run with, I gave you those wings to fly with."

Like the dove, we have a tendency to assume that everything new that comes into our life is exactly like, or similar to, other things that have come into our lives. All the dove knew was running. She didn't know she could do something completely different—fly.

The Torah and the commandments are wings to fly with. But if people pick up the Torah with no real understanding of what it is offering—and if their expectations are that the Torah is somehow similar to everything else they've read before— then they are going to miss its point.

I've seen visitors enter a yeshiva, a place of Torah study, and not understand why the students were so happy. They themselves had read the Torah, but they didn't find it so enjoyable. This feeling is similar to walking into a 3-D movie without the little plastic glasses. Everybody at the movie is saying, "Wow, great!" and the person without the glasses is bewildered, "What's going on here? The picture is distorted." Learning Torah without knowing what it offers is like viewing a 3-D movie without the plastic glasses; something's wrong there.

NOT SO SIMPLE

A rabbi who runs a large yeshiva for women in Jerusalem was once on a plane, sitting next to a world-renowned professor of astrophysics, a Jewish fellow. The professor turned to the rabbi, who also had a PhD but in Jewish education, and he said, "Rabbi, I believe all of Judaism can be summed up in a few words."

The rabbi looked at him in surprise. "Really?"

"Yes, don't do unto others what you would not have them do unto you."

The rabbi stroked his beard for a bit and then responded, "You know, professor, I think all of astrophysics can be summed up in a few words."

"Really?" the professor asked.

"Yes," said the rabbi. "Twinkle, twinkle little star, how I wonder what you are."

Torah is not so simple that one can sum it up in just a few words, because Torah is much more than truth. Torah is life.

To understand the Torah, you can't just read it or study it like other books or subjects. You need to experience it, you need to immerse yourself in it, you need to live it. And to know how to live it you need a teacher.

However, Maimonides, the great Torah scholar of the twelfth century, known as the Rambam, states that one should not pay to study Torah.[1] Indeed a verse from Deuteronomy (33:4) states, "The Torah of Moses is an inheritance for the community of Jacob." You don't pay for an inheritance—it's yours.

Maimonides, however, notes that if you can't find someone who has the time to teach you Torah for free, you are permitted to compensate him, based on the verse in Proverbs (23:23) that states, "Buy truth."[2] But, then Maimonides cautions that if you do end up having to pay to learn Torah, you should not think that you have the automatic right to teach Torah to others for pay.

This sounds a little strange. Why would Maimonides assume that a person would be so obnoxious as to say, "I paid, so now somebody better pay me, too"?

I believe there's something more to what Maimonides is saying: Torah is not just truth. It's something much greater than truth. Maimonides is saying that when you pay for your Torah study, then you only receive the truth of it, because you can buy truth. But you can't buy the life of Torah.

There is a distinct difference between truth and life. Truth is information; life is experience. No one can transmit life to you by virtue of communicating information. You can study truth. But to experience and encounter life you have to get involved. You have to immerse yourself in it. You have to taste life. For example, I can tell you the truth about chocolate cake: it's made of cacao, sugar, eggs, and flour. But you will experience chocolate cake only if you taste it. The same goes for Torah. You can't just read it or study it—you have to get involved with it. More than truth, Torah is a living encounter with God. The revelation of God at Mt. Sinai wasn't simply an opportunity for the Jewish people to receive truth. What happened at Mt. Sinai was a face-to-face encounter with God in real time. It wasn't just the transmission of information that was important, it was the meeting with the living God, the one who is the life of all life.

Someone can tell you everything you'd like to know about your potential spouse, but until you meet the person you merely have some facts. When you do meet, there will be an exchange that you won't be able to capture in concepts or words. Similarly, the experience at Mt. Sinai was not only a revelation of God's truth; more importantly, it was a revelation of God's love.

To access that revelation 3,300 years later requires a deep commitment to learning Torah. Only through our involvement with the Torah's text can we hear God's voice, feel His divine presence, and experience God's love as our ancestors did at Mt. Sinai. Because getting involved with the Torah is a living encounter with God, the author.

To learn Torah, you have to get involved with its author through the text. Other books you can just read or study at arm's length. In fact, most of the time when you read a book you know next to nothing about the author and you are generally not so interested in getting to know him. You simply want the story, ideas, or facts contained in the book. But that is not possible to do with the Torah.

The oral tradition tells a story of a rabbi who said to his friend, "You know, had I gotten to class earlier I would have known double what I know today."

Shocked, his friend asked, "Were you really so late that you missed half the class?"

The rabbi responded, "No, I arrived before the teacher started, but the room was already so full that I had to sit behind him. Had I seen his face, I would have known double what I know today."

Through this story, the oral tradition is teaching us an important lesson: Torah knowledge is not just about amassing ideas and facts. To know Torah is also to connect with the divine spirit within the teacher of Torah. This is also true when we learn the text of the Torah. The more involved we are with it, the better we get to know and connect with its author, God, because only then can we actually hear God speak to us through the text.

THE VALUE OF INTERPRETATIONS

One of the big problems people have with learning Torah is that they become confused with the many different, and sometimes contradictory, interpretations that many commentators offer. What could be the value of learning text that can be explained in so many different ways? Isn't it all subjective and not the absolute word of God?

One of my college assignments was to read *The Great Gatsby*. I remember the teacher asking the class whether we knew the meaning of the phrase "the green light flashing across the bay." I put up my hand and said, "Well, I think F. Scott Fitzgerald was sitting in his cottage and writing this chapter when he looked out of his window across the bay and saw a green light flashing. He liked the way it looked, so he threw it into the scene."

The teacher said, "Wrong, David."

So I said, "But how do you know I'm wrong?"

"Believe me," she replied. "This is a symbolic phrase. The green light means the road is open, but because it is flashing, this implies hesitation, and the water stands for instability and yearning."

But I didn't buy it. "Naah," I said. "He was just sitting in his cottage and he was looking across the bay. Anyway, how could you know what symbols he had in his mind?"

Of course, with this attitude I failed the course.

But it was a good question. When we pick up a book, what right do we have to interpret it? Unless the author tells us what he really intended, how could we know what he meant? Is this not the same problem with the Torah?

For centuries sages have pored over the words of the Torah and offered new and different interpretations. How do we know which ones are right?

With any other book, unless the author tells me what he meant, I do not know for sure what he intended to say. My understanding is simply my subjective interpretation. But when you immerse yourself in Torah, the author, God, personally tells you what He meant.

How so? According to Kabbalah, you are a soul, and that means that the real you is a part of God. Therefore, when you immerse your true self in the Torah, it is as if the author continues to study His own book through you, the reader, because you are actually a part of the author. Therefore, God reveals new meanings of the Torah every day when you immerse yourself in the text.

Every time you get involved with the Torah, you can meet God face to face. And then every interpretation that comes to your mind is a revelation. Therefore, as people open the Torah and get involved with the text, they reveal new facets every single day.

Of course, this does not mean you can just say anything you want and distort the meaning of the text. You must acquire the proper skills and intentions to explore the text with your soul, so that you can open the channel for new revelations. This is possible because Torah isn't simply a book that records an experience that happened 3,300 years ago. Torah is an ongoing revelation that every one of us can connect to. When you open up the Torah and ask a question about the text, when you examine the various commentary and put all the interpretations together, all of a sudden something hits you. You get an understanding, a flash of revelation.

But most people don't know this, because they don't know how to access the book. In fact, one of the fastest ways to turn a person off to Judaism is to have them read "the Bible."

The Gideons International—a Christian group that prides itself on placing worldwide 120 Bibles a minute—decided that every hotel room should have a Bible right next to the bed. But this is not a book you read before you go to sleep. If you really want to understand what God is communicating to humanity, you can't simply *read* it. You have to get to know the author through involvement with His message, using the proper skills and intentions.

The *Zohar* compares involvement with Torah to a loving

relationship between a man and a woman. Initially the woman is behind a wall, waiting to reveal herself to the man. If he proves he is willing to be patient, she comes out from behind the wall, but still hides behind a curtain. And if he continues to wait, she then reveals herself to him through a lattice. It's a beautiful description of how we yearn for a connection that becomes more and more open to us the longer and the harder we try.

In short, the Torah is not something you study; it is something you get involved with. The Torah is not a book; it is a meeting place. Through our involvement with its text we meet God, the author, and begin to see how, through His words, He speaks through us and reveals Himself to us.

At the start of each day a Jew traditionally recites a prayer called *Birkat HaTorah*, the blessing for learning the Torah. The blessing begins, "Blessed are You God, King of the Universe, Who has sanctified us through His commandments, and commanded us *to be immersed* in the words of Torah."

Had God simply commanded us to study Torah, the blessing would have said *to study*. But instead, the blessing uses the Hebrew word *la'asok,* which means to be involved/occupied/immersed. Therefore, we do not study Torah; we immerse ourselves in it.

TORAH AND INDIVIDUALITY

The *Birkat HaTorah* blessing continues: "Please, God, make Your Torah sweet in our mouths and in the mouths of the House of Israel so that we and our children and our children's children will all know Your name and study Torah for its own sake. Blessed are You, *HaShem*, Who teaches Torah to His nation Israel."

The first part of the blessing told us that our approach to Torah must be our desire for involvement. This second part of the blessing is telling us something amazing: that the Torah can be sweet, because God will teach us daily what we need to hear.

But how can the Torah really be sweet? We know that taste is somewhat relative. For instance, my daughter doesn't like candy very much. She likes olives. In the synagogue, when all the kids run to the candy man for chocolates, my daughter looks at him with her big brown eyes and asks, "Don't you have olives?" For her, that's tasty. So what is sweet is relative to our individual tastes.

When we pray for the Torah to be sweet, we're asking God to relate to us as individuals and teach us the Torah we need to hear. People often mistakenly think that Judaism isn't personal. But when we properly learn Torah, we know it supports individuality. Every day that we involve ourselves and experience its revelations, we see how the Torah relates to us personally. That's why the blessing concludes with the reference to God "Who *teaches* Torah," using the present tense.

The part of the blessing that reads, "so that we and our children and our children's children will all know Your name" is telling us what we should be aspiring to achieve through Torah: to know God's name. Our goal is to learn how to call to God, make a connection, and evoke His presence in our lives. Years of Torah study will not teach us how to know God's name; only real involvement in Torah and the understanding that God will relate to each of us personally will enable us to form a real here-and-now relationship with God.

This is what we pray for daily: "Please, make the Torah sweet in our mouths, make it relate to us, so that we get the individual guidance that we need today, so that we can know Your name and connect with You."

7.

Why Pray?

TODAY, very few people really know what it means to
pray.

The extent of my prayer experience as a child was going to
a synagogue with my father on the High Holidays. To me, the
prayers seemed to consist of a lot of mumbling that finished
with a resounding "Amen!" It sounded as if all you had to say
was the first word on the page and the last word on the page.
This made sense to me. After all, why waste God's time? Surely
God has heard these prayers many times and for thousand of
years.

Rabbi Shlomo Carlebach, the famed "singing rabbi," used to
tell a story that aptly describes a child's approach to prayer. As
a young boy, he had locked himself into a room for the morning prayers. After about three hours, his brother finally confronted him about what he was doing in there.

"I was just praying," Shlomo told him simply.

"For three whole hours?" his brother asked incredulously.
"What kind of praying takes three hours?"

"I was reciting the *Shemoneh Esrei*," Shlomo said.

"*Shemoneh Esrei* for three hours?" his brother exclaimed. He knew that it normally takes about ten to twenty minutes to complete this prayer, which is composed of nineteen short blessings. "But I did it thirty times," Shlomo replied. "This way I have my mornings free for the whole month!"

Like the young Rabbi Shlomo, we do not always know what we are doing when we pray. Sometimes it feels like we are simply going through the motions.

When I started revisiting Judaism as a teen and getting more involved, I thought that the faster a person prayed, the holier he was. To reach the goal of being the fastest-praying Jew, I started the "Prayer Olympics" with some friends. We thought that the one who prayed the fastest won God's favor.

In my first year in yeshiva, I realized that I needed to find more depth and meaning in my prayer. So I asked a religious fellow for some advice about prayer. In turn, he asked me if I knew what to do if I was in a strange town and it was time to say the afternoon prayers but I was nowhere near a synagogue. I didn't know. So he explained, "What you should do is go into a telephone booth, open up the phone book, take the receiver in your hand, and pretend to be on the phone with someone while you pray."

He cautioned me to be sure the phone is working because one day, as he was praying in a phone booth, someone started knocking on the door. He was concentrating on his prayers, so he motioned with his hands for the other person to wait. After a few minutes the guy finally gave up. Later that day, as he was walking down the street, he saw the fellow again. He felt bad that he tied up the line so he approached him.

"Excuse me," he said. "I want to apologize for making you wait. I was on a long-distance call."

"You were?" The guy was surprised. "I wanted to let you know that that phone hasn't been working for years."

You can imagine how surprised and disappointed I was when I received such a superficial tip as my advice on how to pray. I asked others for advice but theirs was equally disappointing.

In the end, I realized what my problem was. And therefore I can tell you now that to determine how to pray most effectively and turn the act of prayer into a meaningful and inspirational experience, you must pinpoint exactly what you are trying to accomplish through prayer.

CAN'T FAKE IT

Prayer cannot be faked. When we pray, we are talking to God. We are forced to ask big questions like, "Why am I doing this? Is God really listening, and does He really care?" To really address these issues is a major challenge.

When I was in yeshiva we always prayed the afternoon prayers after a Talmud class and right before lunch. The timing was perfect because we could pray for something good to eat. One day as I was beginning to pray, a little voice came inside my head and said, "David, what are you doing?"

"I am praying," I replied.

"But, David, look how hard you work at analyzing and understanding Talmud. Do you try to understand the meaning of your prayers like you try to understand the Talmud?" the voice prodded.

"Excuse me, would you mind? I am trying to pray," I snapped.

But the little voice kept annoying me and challenging me to pray with *kavanah*, the Hebrew word for "sincere concentration." So I took the preparatory three steps back and three steps forward and started the *Shemoneh Esrei* prayer, the most important prayer of every prayer service.

I barely said, "*Baruch Atah* (Blessed are You)" when I stopped. What does this mean? How can I bless God? Suddenly, my mind started analyzing every word of the prayer as if it were a piece of Talmud, trying to figure out what I was really saying. Everyone in the yeshiva had finished the whole prayer, and I had not even finished the third blessing.

That was when I had a profound mystical experience: I heard a deep growl coming from the center of my being. After a minute, I realized that it was my stomach praying. It knew that if I did not get to lunch soon, there was going to be no food left. So I raced through the rest of the blessings. It was then that I decided to do extensive research on prayer and the Jewish prayer book, the *Siddur*.

Throughout my explorations, I found that the formal liturgy embodied in the *Siddur* is problematic for several reasons. Some people do not understand the Hebrew words, while others do not even understand the English translations. Many people do not understand what they should be feeling during prayer, and some find prayer in a synagogue simply boring.

When I attended synagogue as a child, I thought that the major job of the rabbi was to call out the page numbers. And I felt sorry for him, because he was always trying to keep the congregation from chatting with each other. I recently visited that synagogue decades later and saw the children of these people doing the exact same thing.

The problem with prayer is not the lack of concentration. That is really just the symptom of the true problem. The true problem is that prayer borders on heresy. My teacher once said that if it would not be a mitzvah to pray, it would be forbidden. After all, it is arrogant and philosophically illogical to think we are going to change God's mind.

At first glance prayer seems to be about whining and begging God, "Please heal this person, please bring me my soul mate, please help my business," and so forth. One could mistakenly think that God is holding out on us and gets pleasure from watching us grovel.

When we are faced with very serious problems, it is customary to ask others to join together in our prayers. What is that all about? It seems as if we hope to move God through force: "God, if you don't respond to my prayers, I will get all of Jerusalem to the Western Wall to pray. And if that's not enough I will recruit thousands of others through e-mail to pray until you hear our prayers."

Do we think these strategies really work? What are we actually doing here? If God is all knowing, then why am I telling Him my problems? He already knows them. If God is good, then why am I asking Him to change my situation? Obviously, whatever happens to me is for my good, and I should just trust God.

To appreciate what we are actually doing when we pray, we have to examine what prayer really means.

THE TRUTH ABOUT PRAYER

First, we have to understand that in Judaism we do not pray. Prayer is an English word, which actually comes from the Latin word *precari*, meaning "to beg"—exactly what most people think about prayer. They imagine a big king in the sky who is getting a big ego boost from watching his subjects beg. This is a terrible image of ourselves and of God. What Jews do when they come to pray is *l'hitpallel*—a unique experience, which as with most Jewish things today, has been distorted by the wrong Western connotation.

L'hitpallel has nothing to do with begging God to change His mind. *L'hitpallel* is a reflexive verb, and it means to do something to yourself, not to God. When you are praying, your question should not be, "Is God listening to my prayers?" Rather, you should ask yourself, "Am I listening to my prayers? Does what I hear impact me? Have I changed?"

If you are under the impression that praying is communicating to God information that He does not already know, then the whole prayer experience becomes ridiculous. God knows that your business is falling apart. God knows that you desperately want your soul mate. God knows exactly what is going on in your life.

L'hitpallel is not about getting God to listen. It is about you hearing your prayers. You need to say these things to God, because you need to hear yourself saying them. In fact, the main requirement of praying the *Shemoneh Esrei*, the primary prayer in Judaism, is to pray softly enough so that you are the only one who can hear it.

In short, *l'hitpallel* means to do something to yourself. Precisely what you are doing is *palleling* yourself. And what exactly is that?

We see the word *pallel* in the story of Jacob and Joseph. When Joseph learns that his father Jacob is nearing his death, he goes to his father for a blessing for his two children. Jacob says, "I never *pallelti* that I would ever see your face again, and God has allowed me to even see the face of your children."[1] What do you think the term means here?

I never hoped? I never imagined? I never dreamed? I never anticipated?

The great eleventh century Torah commentator Rashi explains the verse to mean, "I never filled my heart to think the thought that I would ever see your face again." Therefore, when we *l'hitpallel*, we are actively, intentionally trying to fill our hearts to think the thoughts with what it is that we want to see in this world, and how we want to change ourselves in order to make these things happen. If we change ourselves, we change our whole situation. It is not God whom we are trying to change. It is ourselves and our relationship to God we are trying to change through prayer.

WILL POWER

The Kabbalah teaches us that our will is really like a ray of God's will. Before God created the universe, all that existed was an endless light. One interpretation is that the endless light is really endless divine will. And human beings are given a thin ray of that endless divine will.

Whatever we do is a result of our will. Without will nothing happens. (For example, you must have the will to read this book.) Will is your life source. When people have tremendous will, they have tremendous life power. Conversely, when people lose their will to live, they can die. I have heard stories about people who have died one day after their spouses died. Their meaning in life centered on their spouses, and when they lost their life's meaning, they lost their will to live. So the will to live is life itself.

One of the most important things that we must do for our children is to give them will power. It is the source of everything. Without will, it is not possible to succeed—or even to proceed—in life.

Prayer is an exercise of will. If you do not use it, you lose it. Ultimately, what we should be doing with our will is exercising it. *Kavanah* is not only sincere intention but attunement of our will to the source of all wills—God's will.

In a book called *Shaarei Orah*, the great thirteenth century master of Kabbalah, Rabbi Joseph ben Abraham Gikatilla, wrote that people do not succeed in their prayer because they have not come to know the true source of all will. When a person really understands and connects with the source of all will, his or her prayers are answered.

But who is answering whom? When we pray we are attuning our will to God's will. Our goal in prayer is to channel God's will, not change it. Our will, in fact, becomes a channel for God's will so that it can become manifest in the world.

GOD'S WILL

Prayer, therefore, actually attunes our will to what our inner self really wants. But what *should* we want? What is really worth wanting? One of the sad tragedies of the world today is that often we don't know what we want. Worse still, there are crafty marketers out there who make it their job to convince us what we want. "You definitely want that car, you can't do without it." "You have to have that new plasma TV." Without clear direction, and bombarded daily by commercial advertising, we are simply confused. And this is where the *Siddur* comes in; it helps us get in touch with what is worth wanting—what God wants.

The Talmud describes a sage who was known for his incredible powers of healing through prayer. The sage would say, "I can tell when my prayer succeeded because the words were sent into my mouth." How well his words were attuned to God's determined his success. Similarly for us, what we should be trying to do in prayer is to pray God's prayer. God wants us to bring His prayer into the world through our will. In doing so, we do more than recite the prayer; we *become* the prayer.

Becoming the prayer is what it means to have *kavanah*. Although translated as sincere concentration or intention, *kavanah* really means attuning ourselves to God's will. This is a little bit like tuning a radio. Right now there may be sound waves passing through the room, which means that music is playing in the room; but if we don't tune in the radio, we will not hear it. In the same way, we must attune ourselves to pray God's prayer. When we pray we are not trying to change God's will; we are trying to *channel* God's will. God only wants good for us. But it is up to us to channel that good will into the world so that it becomes actualized.

The Kabbalah teaches us that not only is our will a channel for God's will, it is actually the vessel to receive the abundant blessings that God wants to give us. Judaism teaches that God's abundance is always flowing, but we have to be ready and willing to receive it and not block it out.

How to Pray

The Book of Genesis explains why God wants our prayers:

> These are the generations of the heavens and of the earth when they were created, in the day that God made the earth and the heavens, and every plant of the field before it was in the earth, and every herb of the field before it grew; for God had not caused it to rain upon the earth, as there was not a man to till the ground.[2]

God had not sent down rain for plants to grow, because there was no one to work the field. As the Midrash explains, there was no human being to recognize the goodness of rain, and thus to pray for it. In order for God to bring rain, God needed a human being to pray and want the rain.

Examining this concept, the Kabbalah describes that an

arousal from below precipitates an arousal from above. God cannot pour blessings upon us until we arouse ourselves to want to receive those blessings. For example, our desire to be healed becomes the vessel for receiving the healing. Our desire for our soul mate becomes the vessel to receive our soul mate. God may have wanted to give you your soul mate long ago, but He may be waiting for your prayer. The same holds true for human relationships: if I give you something that you do not want, I did not really give you anything. Yet the more you want something, the sweeter and more beautiful it is when I do give it to you.

Imagine you want to surprise your friend with a gourmet dinner, so you tell him to come over at seven. He thinks, "Hmm, seven, that's dinnertime. But I guess he wants to speak to me about something important." On his way over, he thinks that since he can't focus well on an empty stomach, he will grab a quick bite and fills up on a burger and fries. When he gets to your house, you yell, "Surprise!" and point to the incredible gourmet meal in the dining room. What will your friend do? He will eat the meal so as not to hurt your feelings, but he will not enjoy it, because he is not hungry. In the same way, God cannot give us something unless we are hungry. In fact, God sometimes orchestrates our hunger so that we will thirst for His blessing. And does it ever taste good when we get it, because we are so ready for it.

Everything in your life is happening because God is stimulating your will and guiding you to clarify what you want. Every day God is helping you realize that what you *really* want is what

He wants to give you and that you are deeply interested in receiving these blessings. God is building your will so that you
will have a big enough vessel to receive what you truly and
deeply want.

The story of the Jewish matriarchs is an excellent example
of this concept. Sarah, Rebecca, and Rachel all had fertility
problems, and therefore they prayed intensely for children.
Giving birth to a child is one thing, but giving birth to leaders
of a nation requires a refined, expanded will. All the waiting,
yearning, and praying prepared them for bringing great souls
into the world—the progenitors of the Jewish nation.

Growing up, I used to listen to the rock star Janis Joplin. She
sang a song that was a satire about prayer: She asked God for a
Mercedes Benz because her friends all drove Porsches.

What do you want, a Mercedes Benz? And why do you want
it—because your friends have Porsches? The matriarchs could
not have wanted children simply because their friends had
children. They had to clarify *why* they really wanted children,
because the children that God was ready to give them were so
historically significant that they had to have the right will to
receive them.

We must constantly ask ourselves how much do we really
want what we ask for, why do we want it, and how ready are we
to receive it?

The standard advice of Kabbalists to people who are praying
for their soul mate is to buy your future bridegroom a *tallit*
(prayer shawl) or your future bride Shabbat candlesticks even
though you have not yet met him or her. Why? To arouse your

will and anticipation. You so much want to meet your soul mate that you are already preparing for the wedding.

Remember, we are praying for our own sake: to channel God's will and to change ourselves. But we are also praying for God's sake. God wants us to want His will. Until we want the abundant blessings that God wants to give us, God cannot give them to us. And He is waiting patiently, because it seems that all we want are mansions, big jobs, and fancy cars. He has so much more to give us, and this is all that we want.

A story is told about a Hassidic rebbe who needed to get to a certain town before Shabbat, so he hired a horseman to get him there on time. The horseman was very conscientious about his job and worked very hard to fulfill the rebbe's request. They ran into a storm, so the horseman had to drive his horse very hard to get to the town on time. When they arrived, the rebbe blessed the horseman that he should get a big portion of spiritual abundance in the world-to-come. A few days later, the horse died from the stress of the trip, and the horseman was so heartbroken over the loss of his horse that he also died. When the horseman arrived in the world to come, God fulfilled the rebbe's blessing and gave the horseman a big portion, but this portion did not interest the horseman. All he wanted was his horse; he missed his horse and was unhappy in the world-to-come. So God decided to give him a new horse, and they rode the trail for eternity.

The horseman could have had an incredibly meaningful portion in the world-to-come, but he did not have the vessel to receive it. Sometimes what you want is all that you can get.

Clarifying our will and becoming the vessel to receive God's blessings is what prayer is all about. A great example of this process is the story of the Wizard of Oz. Dorothy does not appreciate home. All of a sudden, she is thrown far from her home, exiled, only to realize that there is no place like home. The only one who can get her home, she learns, is the Wizard of Oz, who lives at the end of the yellow brick road. Along her travels, she finds friends who all need something from the Wizard because he, they believe, can give them everything they want.

Like in every good story, there is the antagonist, the wicked witch, who challenges and frustrates Dorothy every step of the way. But in the process the witch gives Dorothy the opportunity to determine how much she really wants to go home, and what she is willing to do to get there. Finally, Dorothy gets to the Wizard, who has a balloon that can take her home. She is so excited. But something goes wrong and the Wizard's balloon takes off without Dorothy.

At this point, the good witch, Glinda, shows up as the savior. Dorothy is crying her eyes out and Glinda is smiling sweetly. Glinda says to Dorothy, "No problem. All you have to do is click your heels three times and say, 'There's no place like home.'"

As a kid, I got very upset at this point. If I were Dorothy, I would have turned to Glinda and said, "Where have you been all this time? Couldn't you have come a little earlier, like before the flying monkeys? Do you know how much money I will have to spend on therapy to get those monkeys out of my head?"

I later realized that Glinda could not have shown up until Dorothy was ready to *say* wholeheartedly that there was no place like home. She had to clarify what she wanted, just as many of us need to clarify what we want.

CREATING OUR WORLD THROUGH PRAYER

Prayer is not only an exercise in clarifying our will but also an exercise in adjusting our vision. It affects not only what we want for ourselves and the world but also the way we see the world, because we actually live in the world of our perceptions.

With our thoughts and attitudes, you and I, at this very moment, are creating the world in which we live. A group of people in the same room can actually be in different rooms. One person can walk into the room, feel disgusted, and say, "I hate the cheap panelling on that wall." Another person can come in, feel cold, and say, "The air-conditioning is on too high here." And another may feel inspired and say, "I love the art on the walls." Objectively they are in the same room, but subjectively they are in very different rooms. Their perceptions create their worlds.

So too, in order for God to be part of our world, we must open our eyes to Him. We must acknowledge and invite God into our world; otherwise, He will not be in our world.

Rabbi Shlomo Carlebach used to tell a story that illustrates this principle. On his way to a belated bar mitzvah of a fellow who had become religious as an adult, he had a confrontation with the man's mother. An atheist, the woman was angry at her son's new religious lifestyle. She wondered bitterly where she had gone wrong. She had done the best she could for her son to live a true and happy life, and now look at him. Angry and frustrated, she turned to Rabbi Carlebach, "I don't believe in God."

He looked at her and said, "So don't believe in God."

She was shocked. "How can you say that?" she said. "You are a rabbi!"

"If you don't believe in God, then don't believe in God," he repeated. Until then, every religious person she had talked to had argued with her. Rabbi Carlebach was the first person—a rabbi, no less—who said that if she did not believe in God, fine.

Intrigued, she asked him, "What do you mean by that?"

"Listen, if you want to live in a godless world, then go ahead. That is your choice. If you don't want to see God in your life, He will not be in your life. Even though God is certainly in your life, you won't see Him."

We create the world in which we live. That does not mean that we create reality—God is the ultimate reality—but our perception of God will determine whether we experience Him in our lives or not. If we are color-blind, we live in a world without colors. And if we are God-blind, we live in a world without God. God is, so to speak, the Master of the Universe and all is under His loving guidance, but if we do not acknowledge that to be true, we will not experience that truth.

Through prayer we acknowledge God. The more we pray to God and thereby acknowledge His love and care for us, the more His love and care become manifest in our life, so much so that our very world is transformed. When we praise Him and His wonders, we enable these wonders to become part of our perceptual world, not just our spiritual world, but also the very world of our senses.

Our eyes, ears, nose, mouth and touch receive raw data from our surroundings. Then our mind, which operates like the hard drive of a computer, organizes that data into the picture that we see. This is how the world appears to us. An animal may not see the world the way we do, because its mind may organize the raw data differently.

Judaism claims that if you were to add God-consciousness to the hard drive of your mind, then your mind would organize the data differently and your world would be different.

The Talmud tells us a story about Rabbi Chanina ben Dosa, whose daughter mistakenly bought vinegar instead of oil for her Shabbat lamp. She realized her mistake only minutes before Shabbat began and was saddened that she could not light her lamp. When her father walked in she explained to him her problem, but he said, "Don't worry. He Who said oil shall light can say vinegar shall light. So light the vinegar my love." She did so and miraculously the vinegar lit like oil.

In Rabbi Chanina's mind, God's power was obvious and that truth manifested itself in the world he lived in. For him the natural was miraculous, and therefore, the miraculous was natural.

All of Judaism—its teachings and lifestyle—transforms the hard drives of our minds and creates for us a new world of miracles. And prayer helps bring that world into daily focus.

In short, prayer makes of us a vessel to receive God's blessings. It builds our awareness of God, and the more we acknowledge God and the more we invite Him into our world, the more we experience His divine presence in our daily lives.

8.

Why Celebrate Shabbat?

WHAT SHABBAT REALLY IS and how Jews perceive it are often two different things.

An experience I had working with a Jewish youth group describes just how true this is. I was hired to try to rejuvenate interest in Judaism among the participants, and I thought a "Shabbat Experience" would be a great idea. So I presented my plan to one of the group leaders, a girl of about sixteen. She looked at me in total shock. "Shabbat!?!" she exclaimed. "Do you mean no tearing toilet paper?" This was the first thing that came to her mind. When I said "Shabbat," she thought "toilet paper."

So in jest I said, "Yes! Haven't you ever tried that? For thousands of years, Jews get together, put a roll of toilet paper on a table, sit around the table and chant, 'Don't tear it, don't tear it!'" She looked at me with an expression that said, "Is this guy for real?" And then she said, "You know, I always wanted to ask a rabbi, 'Are you allowed to flush on Shabbat?'"

Imagine, this is *the* question she always wanted to ask a rabbi.

Perhaps partial ignorance is an even greater problem than complete ignorance. At least when we know nothing, we don't have bad feelings. But partial ignorance can translate into a total distortion. It would have been better for the girl to be completely ignorant of the laws of Shabbat observance than for her to think of toilet paper in association with the most beautiful of Jewish celebrations. As a result she is not even open to experience an authentic Shabbat.

Like this girl, most Jews know what you *don't* do on Shabbat: you don't drive, you don't write, you don't turn on lights, you don't shop, and so forth. But they don't know why, and what's more, they don't know what you *do* on Shabbat.

Of course, when you focus only on what you don't do on Shabbat, an experience which is supposed to be joyous and fulfilling ends up sounding like torture. You have to ask yourself, "Is this the way I want to celebrate a holiday? Is this how I want to spend my weekend after working hard all week long?"

When I was in high school, before I got involved in Judaism, my sister began keeping Shabbat. Of course, I thought she was insane. For me it seemed that keeping Shabbat was a waste of a perfectly good Saturday. At the time, I was in a rock band that used to practice on Saturdays at my house. The guys would come over with their amps and electric guitars, and we'd have a good time practicing. To me, Saturday meant having a good time.

But to my sister, Saturday was different: it was Shabbat. She would get up early in the morning and go off to the synagogue, and she would enjoy the tranquility of this holy day. Meanwhile, my friends and I would be hanging out and rehearsing songs like the Rolling Stone's "Sympathy for the Devil" and other equally inspiring songs. Once when I heard my sister

walk up to the door of the house on her way home from synagogue, I said to my friends, "Shhh guys, it's Shabbat, and my
sister's coming home." As she opened the door we gave her this
electrifying "GOOD SHABBOS!" My sister, of course, was
not impressed and was actually very annoyed. At the time, I
just thought she was being a crazy religious Jew, and I was being
a rotten brother, and isn't that the way a brother-sister relationship is supposed to be.

Sometimes, she would get a phone call from a friend, and I
would say "Hedy, the phone's for you," and she would say, "You
know it's Shabbat, you know I can't use the phone."

"Would you like me to say that?"

"No, you shouldn't use the phone either!"

"Well, then what should I do? Your friend is waiting on the
line."

Then I'd ask her questions like "Isn't it true that you're not
allowed to turn on electricity?"

And she'd say "Yes, that's right."

I'd say, "Uh huh, so are you allowed to walk on Shabbat?"

She'd say, "Of course, it's relaxing to walk."

So I'd say something like, "Wait a second, when you're walking are you not creating electrical friction by moving your feet
along the ground, and isn't that electricity?"

But while I would think up these really obnoxious questions
to annoy her, I'd actually wonder about the logic of the dos and
don'ts of Shabbat.

In order to understand that logic—and by extension the real
meaning of Shabbat—let's look at the first place it is men-

tioned in the Torah. This paragraph is from the Book of Genesis,[1] and it is recited every Friday night at the start of Shabbat dinner, as part of a blessing over wine called *kiddush*:

And it was evening, it was morning, the sixth day. And heaven and earth were completed and all their hosts. And God completed on the seventh day the work that He created to do, and God refrained on the seventh day from the work that He created to do.

This statement seems as contradictory as it is cryptic. But it is neither, as we will see.

First of all, it is common knowledge that God created the world in six days, and on the seventh day He rested. According to these words, however, it sounds like God did do something on the seventh day, as it says, "and God *completed* on the seventh day, the work that He created." But had it not been previously stated that "it was evening, it was morning, the sixth day, and heaven and earth *were completed*"? If God finished His work on the sixth day, what was left to do on the seventh day?

According to Rashi, the world was still missing something— rest. Therefore, only then, on the seventh day, when God rested from the work of creation, was it, in fact, finished and completed. In other words, when God rested on the seventh day, this retroactively completed the work of the six days. The very fact that God abstained from activity on the seventh day is what enabled everything that had happened during the six days to become a whole and complete act of creativity.

To understand this concept of retroactive completion, we need to understand the meaning of the Hebrew word for "work" used here, *malacha* ("creative work"), and how this activity differs from other kinds of work, such as "physical labor."

CREATIVE WORK

What you're not allowed to do on Shabbat is *malacha*; but physical labor is actually permitted on Shabbat. In fact, keeping Shabbat does not mean that you can't do anything which involves physical exertion, like moving a chair or a table, for instance.

Generally people understand Shabbat as being a day of rest, but sometimes on Shabbat you get really tired, because you are walking a long way to the synagogue, or you're having many guests to dinner, or doing other things to make your guests and family happy. All these activities can be more physically exhausting than flipping on a light switch. Therefore, *malacha* is clearly not a function of physical exertion. In fact, it has very little, if anything, to do with physical exertion. Rather, *malacha* has to do with creativity. It's called *malachat machshevet*, meaning "action of the mind." Therefore, this kind of "work" refers to a creative act born out of intention and thought.

What determines if an act is a creative act or merely physical labor? The deciding factor is whether I am able to start and stop. If I can't start this activity and if I can't stop this activity, then basically I'm a mindless, compulsive, laborious slave. I'm simply a robot on auto-drive. That's the difference. Creativity is an act of mind and intention. Creativity is something I start doing, and creativity is something I can stop doing at will. I am in control. If I start a creative act, but I can't stop, then it is no longer creativity; it is a mindless, laborious, compulsive activity. I become a victim of some kind of force that's carrying me, rather than a master of my actions directed by my will and intention.

When we celebrate Shabbat, we are saying that God stopped the work that he had done, which retroactively indicates that God also started the work. Therefore, the work that he had done was an act of creativity; the world was a complete creation. While some might claim that either the world has always existed or the world is just an expression of laborious, mindless, natural laws, there is, in fact, a third possibility: that the world is an act of creation, an expression of divine will and intent. And that's the key difference.

Do I choose to believe in a world that is merely a product of blind, laborious, natural forces, or do I choose to believe that the world is the intentional expression of a mindful and willful power—God?

If I live in a world that is the product of intention, if I live in a world that was meant to be, then I live in a meaningful world. A world that wasn't meant to be is not a meaningful world. A world that is simply the product of blind natural forces (that somehow came into being) doesn't have meaning, because it doesn't have a beginning, it doesn't have an end, it doesn't have direction, and it doesn't have intention.

In the final analysis, I decide how I choose to perceive our world.

When I recite the *kiddush* on Friday night and affirm that the world was completed on the seventh day, I am testifying that the world is a creation, which means it is meaningful, it is purposeful, it has a theme, it has direction. It means that I believe the world is an expression of creativity and not simply the mechanistic outcome of natural laws. I believe that the world is not the product of nature at work but the creative masterpiece of God.

To know this truth and to celebrate it every seven days changes my whole week and my whole life. When I stop on Shabbat and refrain from doing the creative activity of *malacha*, I renew the image of God in which I've been created. Otherwise, I am merely an animal compelled and propelled by my natural instincts, rather than a being created in the image of God who has a free will, who has a mind, who has the ability to choose.

Some people can't stop. They don't know how to take a rest. They don't know how to put aside what they're doing. They're compulsive. These are not creative people engaged in *malacha*; these are people who labor. They are slaves to their jobs and slaves to their instincts.

I once saw an animated cartoon about Shabbat produced by an organization called Gesher. It portrays a very busy day in Manhattan, a lot of noise and a lot of traffic, and you see a policeman in the middle of all this traffic, but he doesn't have a face, he has a whistle for a head. A lot of people are walking down the street, but nobody has a face: one fellow has a computer monitor for a head, another has a pen for a head, and another has a wrench for a head. It is a faceless world. Everyone has become his or her career. They are no longer people *with* careers, they *are* careers. There's a feeling of tension and every so often you see a clock that is ticking toward some set time. One fellow, who has a briefcase for a head, is shown walking quickly home. When he finally reaches his home, he enters, sits down in a soft chair, and an alarm clock rings. At that moment his briefcase head melts into a radiant and warm smiling face, and he joyfully says, "Shabbat Shalom."

This cartoon points out that I can lose my humanness. I can become my career. If I become my career, then my career leads me, and I'm just a victim of a mechanistic world; I'm just another cog in a big machine called planet Earth. But Shabbat is the antidote to mechanism. Shabbat is the antidote to the notion that the world is simply some big machine constantly in motion. When I stop on Shabbat, I demonstrate that I am not a compulsive, laborious, mindless bundle of nerves and tissue, but rather I am a human being created in the image of God, and I make my own choices.

I have a friend who is an extremely successful businessman. Once he was working on a big deal to purchase a major company. There were all kinds of complex negotiations going on and for some reason the deal ended up in court. The arguments went on for a couple of days, and come Friday, it was far from over. An hour before Shabbat, my friend turned to everybody in the court—the judge, his lawyers, the other people involved in the deal—and he said to them, "It's almost Shabbat and I've got to get home." They said, "Wait, you can't go. We've got a big deal here, and if you leave now you could lose." He decided to wait a little longer, but Shabbat was coming soon. Finally he said, "Listen, you've got to understand, I would rather lose money than lose Shabbat."

He then got into his car and took off. But then he realized that it would take him another fifteen minutes to get home, but he had only five minutes until Shabbat, so he panicked, pulled into a stranger's driveway and knocked on the door. When the owner opened the door, he said to him "Excuse me sir, but I am Jewish and in four minutes Shabbat begins. Would you mind taking care of my Jaguar for a day?" He handed an absolute stranger the keys to his Jaguar and walked the rest of the way home.

In our society, it is quite amazing that someone would walk away from a big business deal and say, "Sorry, I am not a slave to this deal, and if I lose it I don't care. Shabbat is more important to me."

When we stop for Shabbat, what we're saying is that we are not natural forces, we are not compulsive automatons acting without control over our lives. We are created in the image of God, and empowered with free choice and intention.

If I can't stop, if I can't let go of driving my car for one day, I don't have the car, the car has me. If I can't let go of my job,

I don't have my job, my job has me. That's what I have to decide: whether I want to become a master of my life or a victim of my life.

(By the way, come Monday, my friend did not lose the deal, though he was certainly prepared to lose it. But as it happened, he came out ahead.)

SHABBAT AND FREEDOM

Besides being a reminder of the act of creation, Shabbat is also dedicated to the remembrance of the Jews' exodus from Egypt. These two themes of Shabbat are in fact related, because the exodus from Egypt and the creation of the world are both about freedom.

Leaving Egypt wasn't simply about escaping slavery and the cruel oppression of the Egyptians. Leaving Egypt was also about escaping an idolatrous orientation to life. Idolatry is the antithesis of Judaism. While people tend to associate idolatry with bowing down to rocks, trees, and statues, that is only part of the equation, and not the essence of idolatry.

Paganism and idolatry are the deification of nature: nature becomes God. According to this logic, God is a force, God is a natural law, God is a universal principle. But God is not a warm, loving, and caring creator who directs the world with will and intention. Therefore, idolatry is completely deterministic. According to its world view, we are prisoners of a big machine ruled by the principles of nature. The greatest danger the Jews had to escape from was the deification of nature.

But Jews have always stood against that. In fact, Abraham,

the first man who rejected this view, was called an *Ivri* ("Hebrew"),[2] the man "on the other side." He gave rise to a family of like-minded people, and it was his great-grandson Joseph who first challenged the Pharaoh of Egypt to think otherwise. The Torah relates in the Book of Genesis how the Pharaoh had a dream about seven lean cows and seven fat cows, followed by a dream about seven lean stalks of wheat and then seven fat stalks of wheat. He woke up in a panic and asked his dream interpreters to help him decipher the meaning of his dreams, but none of them could do this to his satisfaction; their answers seemed false and contrived.

Fortunately, one of the people working for Pharaoh suddenly remembered a man named Joseph, a Jewish dream interpreter who was in prison at the time. Pharaoh ordered Joseph to be brought into the palace, and he related the dreams to him. When the Pharaoh had finished, Joseph said, "These dreams are about economics. These dreams are about agriculture. They are telling you that there will be seven good years of plenty followed by seven bad years of drought and famine." The Pharaoh immediately knew Joseph was right.

After he had finished explaining the dream, Joseph, in a bold display of chutzpah, laid out a brilliant economic plan to save Egypt from the impending famine.

This whole story may seem a bit bizarre. How could the finest dream interpreters of Egypt, who were living in an agricultural society, miss the most obvious interpretation about dreams dealing with wheat and cows? What was it about Joseph that enabled him to see so clearly the message in Pharaoh's dreams?

In Egypt, the Nile was a god, because it was the source of all agricultural wealth. The Nile had a very consistent natural pattern of overflowing its banks and irrigating the area. Nobody among the Egyptians could offer an interpretation like Joseph offered, because such an interpretation was the very antithesis of idolatry. It was heretical. Those who deified nature could not say that nature was going to suddenly stop. The Nile had been flowing along its natural course, in a regular pattern for thousands of years, and the Egyptians couldn't imagine that it could ever change. But Joseph knew that nature is not God. His interpretation was a direct message to the Egyptians from the one and only God that nature isn't necessarily consistent, nor is it reliable. Nature must answer to a higher power—its creator—because only He can stop and start at will the natural processes of the world.

The deification of nature is also the deification of man's animalistic drives, the perfect excuse to do whatever comes "naturally" to us.

The ultimate moral implications of idolatry were demonstrated to us by Nazi Germany. Hitler was a pagan, who boldly stated:

> Yes, we are barbarians! We want to be barbarians! It is an honorable title. . . . Providence has ordained that I should be the greatest liberator of humanity. I am freeing men from . . . the dirty and degrading self-mortifications of a false vision [a Jewish invention] called "conscience" and "morality."[3]

"On the other side" stands the Jewish message to the world that human beings are not just animals. We are not victims of our wild instincts. Nature doesn't rule us, and therefore, not only can we transcend nature, we *must* transcend nature. We have free will; we were created in the image of God. We mirror the ultimate reality—God—who is beyond nature, and therefore we, too, can transcend nature.

Nazism, however, deifies nature. Whenever the Nazis felt like killing, they killed. They did not want to stop their "natural" feelings. This is also the reason they didn't believe in miracles: miracles transcend nature.

A student of mine, a physician in her sixties, once approached me and said, "You know Rabbi, my whole life I never believed in God. I never believed in miracles. Then, one day last year, something happened to me and I realized I was wrong."

"So what happened?" I asked.

She explained that while volunteering in Africa, she was treating a person with a terminal disease, who had absolutely no chance of survival, but all of a sudden one day, while looking at a blood sample under the microscope, the disease literally disappeared before her eyes. As she put it, "It was a scientific impossibility. It was a miracle."

Every Shabbat I affirm that this world is a miracle, the free creation of a free creator. I affirm that I am created in the image of God—and that I, too, am free. What I am doing on Shabbat is not simply refraining from turning on the lights. I am celebrating freedom. I am celebrating the fact that nature is not God, but God is transcendent of nature, the source of nature, and the power that controls nature and can bring about miracles.

UNFINISHED BUSINESS

The Midrash says that when God "completed His work" on the seventh day, He didn't finish everything exactly. It was Friday, it was getting late, and He still had a couple more things to do, but He just stopped. He actually rested in the middle of work.

If you can't stop at any moment in your process, then you are a victim of your process being, carried in its flow. The Midrash is saying that God stopped even before He finished. God didn't have to finish the world, because God can do anything. He is a completely free reality. The fact that God didn't finish the work is what made it an even more complete (so to speak) act of creativity.

If I'm painting a picture and I can't stop in the middle—if I must finish this, or I must finish that—then who's painting the picture? Who's the master of whom? We learn from this teaching that the creation of the world was an act of love, because an act of love is an act that you do at will. It is not an act that you are compelled or forced to do.

God didn't have to create the world, and He did not have to finish it either. God didn't have to create the world as a means to some necessary end. Judaism teaches that God *wanted* to create the world for no reason other than to create the world. He wanted it, and therefore what He did was an act of love.

Therefore, celebrating Shabbat also means celebrating the fact that this world is the free expression of God's love.

The first paragraph of the *kiddush* ends with:

"And God blessed the seventh day and made it holy, for on it He refrained from all His work which God had created to do."

What does "God had *created* to do" mean?

From this verse we understand that what God really created was a world full of work to do. God created work to do. And who's going to do that work? You and me. Now that's a perfect world.

The perfect world for human beings is a world that enables us to participate in creating it. There's something for me to do here. If there was nothing for me to do here, what a boring, sad world this would be. Human beings naturally need to contribute to their environment. If God is a creator, then we, who are created in His image, also need to be creators. God created a perfect world for cultivating creators. There's a tremendous amount of creative opportunity in this world. This is God's gift to us—that there's something creative for us all to do here.

Children know this. At an early stage, children want to help around the house. They want to contribute. I can't tell you the joy (and also the fear) of watching my two-year-old son take the broom and start trying to clean up the kitchen. Although he's swinging the broom around the room knocking things off the shelves, it's wonderful to see the natural tendency of the child being expressed. He, too, wants to do something in his house. Children don't only want to be takers, they also want to be givers. They want to contribute. They want to be creative, too. Unfortunately the parents are neurotic. They say, "No,

don't do that! Oh, don't go near this! Oh, you'll break it, stop!"
And, as a result, their children become passive; they become
frightened to be creative. Yet the child's soul wants to create,
because it is an expression of the creator. God created a world
that offers endless opportunities for creativity. There's a lot of
work to be done on earth, thank God.

Except on Shabbat.

On Shabbat we stop.

STOP IN THE NAME OF LOVE

I stop on Shabbat because if I don't stop on Shabbat, then I
mistakenly think that my life is my business, instead of God's
business, and I am "self-employed." Imagine I'm working in a
company and the company closes on Saturday, but I decide to
go in to work anyway. Why?

The Jewish attitude is that the human being is an agent for
God, and because of this the human being can actually become
an angel (malach) by doing God's creative work (malacha).

In other words, God created a world full of opportunities for
creativity, and He appointed me His agent to complete His creative work. I am part of a huge godly corporation, and I'm
working for the boss. And if the boss closes the business on Saturday but I go in to work just the same, then I am confusing
myself by thinking that I don't need to follow his schedule, his
rules, that this is my business, and I do not work for anyone.

When I don't work on Shabbat, I remind myself that I'm
really working for God. During the week I am empowered by
Him to work on His behalf. I represent God in what I do in this

world. This is a tremendous honor. God has entrusted me to do His job. He could have done it Himself if He wanted to, but He wanted me to do it, so that I could be part of creation and contribute creatively. Yet somehow I could get confused and forget who I'm working for. If that happens, then I am laboring under a very egotistical illusion, believing that I work for myself, and that this creative work is my own, and that this world is mine and nobody else's business.

But when I celebrate Shabbat, I remind myself, "This world is God's business, and I just work here."

That's why Shabbat is referred to as the source of all blessings. If I stop working on Shabbat, I'm affirming that my work throughout the week was for God's sake, and then everything I do is blessed with the status of being holy work.

The sad thing is that many people don't know this. They know that Shabbat is a day of rest, but they know other ways of resting that seem to them to be more relaxing and fun. But Shabbat is not about simply resting. It's about rejuvenating. On Shabbat, you get in touch with who you really are.

There's nothing more exhausting than trying to be who you are not. When you're in a job and you feel it's just not you—even if it's the simplest job in the world and you're making a tremendous amount of money with very little responsibility on your head—then you come home exhausted, because it's not really answering your inner needs. You are not being who you could be.

Judaism says you are a soul, a part of the creator, and therefore you are also a creator. But you do not create for yourself, you create for God. When you realize that, you draw much energy and blessings from God.

There is a great deal of truth in the observation of the early Zionist leader Ahad Ha'am: "More than the Jews have kept Shabbat, Shabbat has kept the Jews."

I don't know where I'd be today without celebrating Shabbat every week. Shabbat restores my self-respect. More so, it brings me back to myself. It reminds me that I'm not alone. After working hard all week long, I could start to feel like I work for myself, that nobody has a vested interest in me. But Judaism says that God has a vested interest in me. He invested a part of His very self in me, and this is my soul. My life matters, and what I do matters, because what I am doing is on behalf of God in a world that was created with intention and meaning.

There's a song called *Lecha Dodi* that is traditionally sung at the very beginning of the Shabbat synagogue service: "Come my beloved to greet the bride, the face of Shabbat we will receive."

What does "the face of Shabbat we will receive" mean? On Shabbat you get a whole new face?

Maybe during the week my face was a briefcase. Maybe during the week my face was a pen, or a computer monitor. But on Shabbat, I get a whole new Shabbat face, a face that reflects the transcendent. On Shabbat, I get a face that reflects God. On Shabbat, I am beaming with the likeness of God. And no feeling in the world can compare to that.

9.

Why Eat Kosher?

THE TALMUD tells a story about the famed author of the *Mishna*, Rabbi Yehuda HaNasi.[1] The rabbi was walking down the street one day when a little calf, which had escaped from a slaughterhouse, ran up to him and hid under his cloak. The rabbi said to the calf, "Go back to be slaughtered, for this you have been created." At this point, a divine decree was issued against him, because he had not shown pity on the creature. As a result, he became sick and suffered for many years, until one day he showed pity on a family of rats and was suddenly healed.

We know that Judaism permits us to eat meat as long as the animal was slaughtered properly, so what did Rabbi Yehuda HaNasi do that was so wrong?

He incorrectly said, "For this you were created." The Talmud is teaching us that, contrary to his declaration, animals were not created for human consumption. The first man and woman ate fruits and vegetables, not animals, in the Garden of Eden. It was only later, after the Flood during the time of Noah, that God allowed human beings to eat meat. The Talmud, therefore, is teaching us that eating meat is not a Torah ideal.

We cannot understand the exact connection between the

sins of humanity and the subsequent permission to eat meat, but we do know that eating meat is a concession that God made. The ideal state of humanity is to be vegetarian.

One suggested reason for this concession is that humanity has an inclination for aggression and cruelty. Humans were not created cruel; they incorporated that characteristic over a period of time. And now that we are challenged with this inclination, we have to figure out how to sublimate it and eventually overcome it.

One way is through the consumption of meat. There is something violent about killing and eating an animal; it is a way of releasing aggression. But most of us crave it. Cravings are really our efforts to express and satisfy a need. Better we satisfy our need for aggression by eating meat than by doing something harmful to people. Of course, it would be best if we did not have the urge toward violence or aggression in the first place, but it is a reality that we now have to deal with and work to overcome.

Judaism does not advocate complete suppression of our negative urges; it prefers to give us outlets to sublimate them while guiding us to gradually overcome them. Therefore, when we crave something, we must satisfy the craving in some way, while working toward kicking the habit.

Take a drug addict, for example. There are two approaches to treating the addiction. One method is cold turkey: just stay off the stuff and go through an excruciating period of withdrawal. The other approach is measured withdrawal, which looks like hospital-sanctioned drug abuse but is really medical intelligence. To wean the addict, the doctors slowly administer, each day, decreasing amounts of the drug until the addiction is gone. If a person who did not know anything about this method walked into the hospital, from his limited perspective, he might erroneously conclude that this place promotes drug abuse as an ideal.

In the same way, there are Torah laws that do not express the ideals of Judaism but exist as a way to reach those ideals. In the case of consuming meat, whether it is to satisfy a craving and sublimate the need for aggression (or for some other divine reason unknown to us), the Torah temporarily allows us to do it in the interest of helping us gradually overcome the urge and become vegetarians.

But people who are already vegetarian should not take pride in thinking that this is a sure sign they are more spiritually and ethically evolved than anyone else. Who knows, perhaps they are expressing their cruelty in other ways that are even more destructive. After all, Adolf Hitler was a vegetarian.

THE IDEAL OF TORAH LAW

Although the Torah spells out for us the goals of life and the way to achieve them, we cannot assume that all the laws written in the Torah represent Judaism's ideals. Sometimes a Torah law expresses only the way to reach an ideal, rather than the ideal itself. There are some laws that even seem to contradict the very ideals that, in actuality, they are helping us achieve.

The Torah is a system of values arranged in a specific hierarchy, according to their priority for the present, with consideration for reaching an ideal in the future. Certain authentic

Jewish values might be temporarily conceded for the good of the future. Only God can decide which values can be temporarily overruled for the purpose of getting us to where we must go. Only God can see the beginning, the end, and the middle of the ethical and spiritual evolution of humanity.

The Talmud states, "God says, 'I created the evil inclination and I created Torah as its antidote'" (Kiddushin 30b). The Torah is an antidote to our negative and destructive inclinations. Therefore, the Torah may sometimes appear to be sanctioning some type of amoral behavior, but in fact, it is simply employing a realistic approach in order to empower people to stop doing what they otherwise may not have had the power to overcome on their own.

Keeping these essential principles in mind, we now can explore the meaning of eating kosher and some of the seemingly odd kosher laws, which permit something less than the ideal in order to help us reach the ideal. We will see that incorporated within these laws are windows to the future.

Although God allowed humanity to eat meat for the first time during the time of Noah, what could be eaten and how was limited. For example, one of the "Seven Mitzvot of the Children of Noah" prohibits eating a limb ripped off from a live animal. God deemed that although humanity needed an outlet for its aggression, this was too much.

As the world evolved, God chose the Jewish people to become ethical models for the rest of the world. Therefore He placed upon them even more restrictions regarding the consumption of meat.

Many of these laws are meant to remind us that we should not feel completely comfortable eating meat, so we cannot eat any kind of meat we want, in any manner we want. Torah law states that we can eat the meat only of birds and animals that are herbivorous but not of those animals that are carnivorous. Judaism adheres to the principle that we are what we eat: an animal's character is infused somehow in its flesh and blood, so we have to be careful about which animals we eat. We want to release and sublimate our violent urges, not fuel and increase them.

The great Kabbalist Rabbi Isaac Luria held that unless we are great Torah scholars we should not eat meat during the week; we should only eat it on Shabbat. Perhaps his reasoning is that an over-consumption of meat could also fuel our violent urges rather than sublimate them.

Sports are a good analogy for this. For many years, researchers hailed sports as a great way for men to release their aggression. Now they are finding that it could be just the opposite; in fact, violence and sexual abuse are very high among sportsmen.

Sports can be tough. Many sports involve kicking or hitting a ball or even another person. The game becomes a formula for aggression. When a person is involved in such a game to the extreme, it becomes his personal ideal. Rather than a way of releasing aggression, the sport can become a way of feeding aggression.

In general, the stringent laws of *kashrut* make meat less available and often more expensive, reminding us that the consumption of meat is not ideal.

HUMANIZING SLAUGHTER

Torah law also dictates how to slaughter the animal. The *shochet* ("slaughterer"), using a special razor-sharp knife, must kill the animal with a single quick stroke against its throat. This type of slaughter ensures a rapid death so that the animal is spared any prolonged suffering. In addition, this method expedites the maximal outpouring of the animal's blood. Torah law does not permit us to consume the blood of an animal.

It is bad enough that we are eating animal flesh, but to consume its blood is going too far. Judaism also teaches us that the animal's soul is connected to its blood. Therefore, we want to refrain from ingesting the animal's spirit.

Not only may we not consume animal blood, we must take care to remove any blood absorbed in the meat. One way to accomplish this is through salting. Another is by roasting the meat over an open fire. Interestingly, some very bloody meat, such as liver, requires both techniques. Salting alone does not get the blood out of liver. You must also broil or roast it over a grill, which draws the blood out.

Throughout history, and even today, many countries have tried to make Jewish ritual slaughter illegal, claiming that it is inhumane. Through testing, they claim that they have found a more humane slaughtering technique—electric shock. By placing sensors on the animal's body, they attempt to show that an animal has a more traumatic death when it is slaughtered with a knife than when it is slaughtered by electric shock.

Of course it is difficult to really know just how much pain an animal is experiencing at the point of death. But for Judaism the issue goes deeper than the intensity of the pain experienced by the animal. The core of the matter lies in the definition of humane.

Doesn't being humane imply maintaining our humanness? What is less humane: a guy in a glass booth going "buzz, buzz, buzz," while killing, with the just a push of a button, hundreds of animals as they pass by on a conveyor belt, or someone who is very conscious of the fact that he is slaughtering animals and doing so very carefully one by one?

Whether the animal is in greater pain with Jewish slaughter is debatable, although Jews do not believe that to be true. But even if we could prove that the animal does experience more pain, there is another, more important value to consider: maintaining the awareness that we are slaughtering animals. We can never feel too comfortable about it. In fact, there is another Torah law that requires that we cover the blood once it pours out of the animal, in order to remind ourselves that we should not feel comfortable with what is going on here. We must never become insensitive to what we are doing and forget that it is not ideal.

A Hassidic tale tells about the kind of sensitivity that the Torah encourages:

A new *shochet* arrived in the *shtetl*, and the great Hassidic master the Baal Shem Tov observed that, when sharpening his knife between slaughterings, the *shochet* would spit on the whetstone. The Baal Shem Tov approached him and said, "Your slaughtering ritual is very different from that of the fellow who was here before you."

"Really?" the man replied. "What's the difference?"

"It's the way you wet your sharpening stone," the Baal Shem Tov said.

"How do I do it differently?" the man asked.

"The other *shochet* used to wet the stone with his tears."

Besides dictating how animals are to be slaughtered, the laws of *kashrut* contain other prescriptions and prohibitions. For example, they prohibit eating meat and milk together. One interpretation suggests that these laws remind us that we really have no right to take meat (which is dead flesh) and milk (which is a symbol of life and nurturing) and feel comfortable mixing them. Doing so indicates very perverted values. Of course, you could say, "I really don't want to think about the values of life and death when I'm eating my cheeseburger." But, the point is, you *should* think about it. Because when you are concerned about the way you eat, you subliminally affect the way you conduct your entire life.

ANIMAL SACRIFICES

Knowing all of this, you may wonder how animal sacrifices, which were an integral part of Jewish worship when the Temple stood in Jerusalem, contributed to our spiritual and ethical growth.

According to some Torah commentators, the sacrifices were another concession by God to human nature and were not an ideal mode of worship. God allowed us to offer sacrifices as a way of expressing our remorse for our transgressions. Ideally, God did not want our animal sacrifices, as the Book of Psalms teaches: "God's compassion is on all His creatures."[2]

Many people who are new to Judaism are very disturbed by the references to the sacrifices in the Torah and the Jewish prayer book. Truthfully I do not see why they should have any more problems with animal sacrifices than they have with buying steaks. At least these sacrifices were offered for a deep spiritual purpose and not to satisfy a base physical need.

As for those who shudder at the very idea of killing animals, whatever the purpose, Maimonides offers hope. In his *Guide for the Perplexed*, he explains that sacrifice was indeed a concession of God to the Jews. The Jews needed an expression of their connection to God that was familiar to them, one that was similar to the culture of their times. Therefore God allowed it to be used as a temporary measure.

Traditional Judaism anticipates with joy the rebuilding of the Temple and the reinstitution of the Temple services. The fact that we do not have a Temple at this point in Jewish history is an indication that we are missing something critical in our spirituality. For this reason, a recurring theme in Jewish prayer is our heartfelt desire for the Temple to be rebuilt.

However, some sages teach that once the Temple is rebuilt, the sacrifices will be slowly phased out. We will at first only slaughter animals for sacrificial purposes, but we will cease consuming them. Then, after a period of time, we will no longer be allowed to slaughter animals even for sacrificial purposes—

we will bring only flour offerings. Eventually, even the flour offerings will become obsolete, and the Temple service will consist only of prayer.

Thus we see that Torah is directing the moral and spiritual
evolution of humanity. Therefore it considers not only where
we are headed in the future, but where we are at present. When
we read the Torah, some of its laws may disturb us. But when
this happens, we must remind ourselves of the purpose of the
Torah. Not all the laws of Judaism represent its ideals. Some of
them may even seem to contradict the very ideals that they are
aiming to achieve. In the case of eating meat, the goal of Judaism is that we return to the ideal state of humanity as it was
in the Garden of Eden and become vegetarians. However, not
all of us are ready for that. There are other moral flaws in our
character that we must fix before we can return to this ideal
state. It is all a matter of timing. Judaism asks us to trust the
creator and master of time. God knows our souls and sets our
goals, and He is always leading us toward our personal perfec-
tion and our certain redemption.

Conclusion

LIVING JEWISH AND LOVING IT

THE *Zohar*, which is a Jewish mystical classic, written two thousand years ago, makes a frightening and harsh prediction. It says that there will come a time when the Jews will relate to Jewish tradition like cows eating grass, and that this generation will bring ruin upon itself. What can this mean? Essentially, the cow chews its cud, meaning it eats grass, regurgitates it, and eats it again. Apparently, as far as the cow's sense of taste is concerned, whether the grass is fresh and green or vomit does not makes all that much difference. The *Zohar* is using this metaphor as a symbol for something that is done mindlessly, that is, without intention.

In Jewish tradition there is a concept called *taamei mitzvot*, which can be translated as "reason for the commandments" and also as "taste of the commandments." In Hebrew, *taam* means both "taste" and "reason," and there is definitely a connection between the two. If an understanding of the reasons behind Jewish tradition is lacking, the performance of various religious rituals can become mindless and tasteless.

Imagine a man who observes Shabbat, but it has no meaning to him, no taste. The only thing that keeps him doing it is guilt, or respect for the tradition, or simply habit. If he does not understand the meaning behind what he is doing, he cannot communicate it to his children, and Shabbat observance is likely to disappear in his family sooner or later, in this generation or the next.

Jews who can't taste Torah observe Jewish law like cows eating grass. They chewed before, they chew now, and they'll chew later because they chewed before. But that's when Jewish continuity starts breaking down. That's when children say to their parents, "Why should I do this? What's the point? This is not interesting. This is restrictive and meaningless." And that's when parents respond, "You should. You must. You have to." Rarely do people respond positively to empty demands; instead, they rebel against them. People respond to what they find fascinating, relevant, inspirational, and meaningful. Most people do what they want, not what they should.

Getting excited about Judaism requires understanding the whys of being Jewish. We're missing the real meaning behind our heritage. And without meaning, tradition becomes stale, and commandments become heavy burdens.

The Torah recounts how, before Moses came down from Mt. Sinai with the first set of the tablets of the Ten Commandments, God told him that the Jewish people had created an idol, a golden calf. Moses wasn't alarmed; he was determined to bring the Jewish people the commandments. But as he descended the mountain and saw the Jewish people dancing and singing around the golden calf, he suddenly threw the tablets down and broke them. Why? Why did he lose his determination?

The answer is that God told him about the golden calf, but God did not tell him that the people were dancing and singing. Moses may have imagined the people sitting beside the golden calf and crying because they had lost hope that their leader would return. Surely they would rejoice as soon as they saw him! Instead they were happy with a golden calf.

Moses recognized that if the people could be happy with a golden calf, they would not comprehend the great gift that he was about to bring them from God. The Talmud explains that as Moses came down the mountain, his horror rising at the scene before him, the letters flew off the tablets. When that happened, the tablets became so heavy that Moses couldn't hold them any longer. When the tablets lost their meaning, they became lifeless rock.

So it is with the Torah. When it ceases to be the book of life it becomes dead weight, just a heavy burden.

When the meaning and the taste of Judaism are lost, then there is no love for it and no joy about being a Jew. When a person whom you love asks you for a favor, it is easy to do it, it's a pleasure. But when you don't like the person, the favor can be the hardest thing in the world because there are no good feelings surrounding it.

Too many Jews do not have good feelings about being Jewish. They don't understand the meaning of it. The Talmud says that when people accept the Torah with joy and happiness, these feelings are guaranteed to be long lasting. But when people accept the Torah with anger or feelings of coercion, though they may observe its commandments for a while, eventually they reject them and everything breaks down.

You Get Back What You Put In

Imagine somebody suggesting to you that you tell your spouse "I love you" three times a day. Sounds like a great idea. You wake up in the morning and start rushing off to work. "Oh, my gosh!" You hurry back and say, "Honey, I love you. See you later."

You're having a busy day, lots of big deals in the works, and it's now two o'clock. Oh, no! You call up your wife and say, "Hey, sweetheart, it's me. I love you. I'll call you later."

You get home exhausted, fall asleep on the couch and—oh, no—it's two o'clock in the morning! You panic, run to the bedroom: "Oh, honey, honey, wake up!"

"What is it?" she asks with alarm.

"I love you, goodnight."

So what would happen if that kind of behavior went on and on? Would it keep you ever mindful of your loved one's presence and significance in your life? Or would it become a burdensome obligation? Is it a good idea to tell your spouse "I love you" three times a day, or is it a bad idea?

The answer to that question is up to you. The intentions that you put into it are what you'd get out of it. If a person says "I love you" with no meaning, no feeling, and no understanding, then those words will get in the way of the relationship.

But it is a truly great idea to tell your spouse regularly that you love him or her. You just have to put a little something into it, a little feeling and understanding. The same thing goes for Jewish living. We have to put a little soul into it. We can have a powerful lamp, but if we don't know how to plug it in, it's not going to turn on. The Zohar offers a great parable for this concept. The Zohar describes the commandments as garments. By itself a garment cannot keep you warm; it can only keep the heat inside your body from escaping. Imagine you have the flu. You can have several blankets draped over you and you still may be shaking. The blanket only reflects your own body heat, gives you back what you put out. If you are cold inside, then nothing you put on the outside is going to help you.

In this way the Zohar is teaching us that the commandments—such as celebrating Shabbat, eating kosher, or doing acts of kindness—can only give back to us what we put into them. The commandments are like garments. They were meant to be put on and not to be a put-off.

Judaism gives us powerful and practical ways to connect to God and each other, ways to express our love and to feel loved. It provides down-to-earth spiritual strategies for living a more complete, joyful, meaningful, and enlightened life. But we have to put a little soul into it. And when we do, our life fills with profound purpose and passion and abundant spiritual pleasure. Judaism offers us the tools so that we can be truly living a joyous life. What a gift.

Notes

CHAPTER 2

1. Anthony Robbins, *Unlimited Power* (New York: Fawcett Columbine, 1986), 55.
2. Psalms 119:86.

CHAPTER 3

1. Exodus 20:2.
2. Exodus 31:16-17.
3. Psalms 16:8.

CHAPTER 4

1. Genesis 3:4.
2. Isaiah 59:2.

CHAPTER 5

1. Leviticus 19:2.
2. Proverbs 3:18, 3:17. This is the order in which these two verses are recited when the Torah reading is concluded in a synagogue.
3. Genesis 2:9.
4. Deuteronomy 30:19.
5. Exodus 32:16.
6. Exodus 19:8, 24:3, 24:7.
7. Exodus 24:7.

CHAPTER 6

1. Deuteronomy 33:4.
2. Proverbs 23:23.

CHAPTER 7

1. Genesis 48:11.
2. Genesis 2:5.

CHAPTER 8

1. Genesis 1:31–2:3.
2. Genesis 14:13.
3. Hermann Rauschning, *Hitler Speaks* (Whitefish, Mont. Kessinger, 2006), 220.

CHAPTER 9

1. Babylonian Talmud, *Bava Metzia* 85a.
2. Psalms 145:9.

Invitation to the Reader

Dear Reader,

Please feel free to write me. It would be an honor and a pleasure to receive your comments and questions.

All the best,
David Aaron

c/o Isralight
25 Misgav Ladach
Old City, Jerusalem
97500 Israel
E-mail: david.aaron@isralight.org

For more information about Isralight seminars, retreats, and articles by Rabbi David Aaron, see www.isralight.org and www.rabbidavidaaron.com

About the Author

RABBI DAVID AARON (www.rabbidavidaaron.com) is a visionary and spiritual educator. He is the founder and dean of Isralight (www.isralight.org), an international organization dedicated to inspiring a renaissance in Jewish life, with programs in Jerusalem, Tel Aviv, New York, Los Angeles, South Florida, and South Africa.

Rabbi Aaron has authored several books, including bestsellers *Endless Light*, *Seeing God*, *The Secret Life of God*, and *Inviting God In*. His books have attracted national media attention, including *Larry King Live* and *E! Entertainment*. He lives in Jerusalem with his wife, Chana, and their seven children.

Rabbi David Aaron has taught and inspired thousands of Jews who are seeking meaning in their lives and a positive connection to their Jewish roots.